THE

JAMES SPRUNT STUDIES

IN HISTORY

AND POLITICAL SCIENCE

*Published under the Direction of
the Departments of History and Political Science
of The University of North Carolina at Chapel Hill*

VOLUME 50

———————————— * ————————————

Editors

HUGH TALMAGE LEFLER, CHAIRMAN

FEDERICO G. GIL

J. CARLYLE SITTERSON

KEENER C. FRAZER

GEORGE V. TAYLOR

THE RECRUITMENT OF CANDIDATES IN MENDOZA PROVINCE, ARGENTINA

By

Richard Robert Strout

Memorial University of Newfoundland

CHAPEL HILL

———— * ————

THE UNIVERSITY OF NORTH CAROLINA PRESS

1968

Printed by the Seeman Printery, Durham, N. C.

THIS BOOK WAS DIGITALLY PRINTED.

PREFACE

This book investigates the recruitment of the legislative-gubernatorial candidates by twelve political parties forming the five major party groupings in the Province of Mendoza, Argentina, during the period from 1962 until 1965. This study tests certain assertions about the social background of these parties' candidates, the selection of these parties' candidates by an oligarchical party leadership, and emerging fundamental changes in the political and elective career pattern in Mendoza Province. The political groupings (and their parties) studied are: the Conservative ideological group of parties (which consists of the Democrat Party); the Radical ideological group of parties (which consists of the Popular Radical Civic Union, the Intransigent Radical Civic Union, the Movement for Integration and Development parties); the Socialist ideological group of parties (which consists of the Argentine Socialist, and Democratic Socialist parties); the Peronist ideological group of parties (which consists of the Tres Banderas, Blanco, Popular Movement of Mendoza, Justicialists, and the Popular Union parties); and the Christian Democrat ideological group of parties (which consists of the Christian Democrat Party). Other minor parties such as the Progressive Democrats or certain Peronist labor parties were not included either because this author could not develop access to their leaders or because he decided that these parties were too small and too insignificant. This investigation includes candidates for provincial deputy, provincial senator, provincial governor and vice-governor, and national deputy recruited by these twelve parties. The candidates for national senators were excluded from this study because they are selected by the provincial legislature, whereas all the former officials are elected by direct popular vote. The elections of 1962, 1963, and 1965 were selected because they were most recent; thus, candidates' own recall of their recruitment was freshest and least likely to be confused with other events.

This type of study is needed because neither North American nor Latin American political scientists have studied the organizational structure and processes of Latin American political parties, despite the need for such studies. Indeed, only two Latin American political parties have been analyzed in published studies by North American political scientists. Studies of Argentine political parties have only analyzed the party's historical development, its major personalities, or its ideology and program by means of the traditional legalistic-historical approach of political science. There have been no studies of organizational structure, nor of organizational process and operation, of Argentine political parties using the newer behavioral approach and techniques of political science. An attempt by José S. Campobassi and others, *Los partidos políticos: estructura y vigencia en la Argentina,* failed to avoid this ideological and historical focus. However, Argentine sociologists, since 1963, have published some valuable studies of political elites in Argentina. José Luis de Imaz's *Los que mandan* is a study of the social characteristics of the major socio-economic-political elites in contemporary Argentina. Silvia Sigal and Ezequiel Gallo's article, "La formación de los partidos contemporáneos: la Unión Cívica Radical (1890-1916)," is an analysis of the social background of the original national leaders of the Radical Civic Union Party during its formation. In 1966 Darío Cantón published *El parlamento argentino en épocas de cambio: 1890, 1916 y 1946,* the only comparative study of the social background of Argentine national legislators during three periods of political crisis and change. Sergio Bagú's *Evolución histórica de la estratificación social en la Argentina* is a study of the formation of Argentine social elites in the period since 1880 with insights into the leadership of the Argentine political parties during this period.

However, the common characteristic of all these studies of political parties and political elites in Argentina has been their focus upon the national level. When these studies have included some mention of events and situations at the provincial level, the concern has been confined to the Province of Buenos Aires. There is no behavioral study of a specific political party or the politics of a specific province in Argentina. The Interior Provinces of Argentina have been neglected in the concerns of political scientists and sociologists.

The only previous study of Mendocino politics is Dardo Olguín's *Lencinas: el caudillo radical,* an historical analysis of the formation of the Radical Civic Union in Mendoza Province during the period 1905-1920. Although an historical study, Olguín's book contains penetrating insights into the organizational structure and organizational process of one major political party in the first part of this century. Knowledge, however, is needed of party process and party actors in an Interior Province, such as Mendoza Province, in the contemporary period.

This book presents this desired knowledge by means of the following format, which naturally divides into three parts. The first division consists of two introductory chapters, which serve to orient the reader. Chapter I fulfills two functions. First, it examines the socio-economic conditions and the cultural factors which determined and influenced the political environment within which the provincial political parties operated. Second, it indicates the political style, and its causes, as practiced by the provincial politicians. Chapter II examines the historical factors which determined the over-all pattern of political party development in

Mendoza Province as well as the pattern of internal development of each political party examined in this work.

The second part, Chapters III through IV, analyzes statistically the data gathered in this investigation. Chapter III examines certain selected socio-economic characteristics of about one-third of all the candidates nominated by these twelve political parties. The purpose of this chapter is to test whether certain political parties nominate candidates having certain socio-economic characteristics, as is commonly asserted by students of the Argentine. Chapter III is concerned to determine the applicability of these assertions only to political party candidates, not to the political party membership or supporters. The method is to classify the candidates into the five major political groupings and to examine each socio-economic variable upon the basis of this classification from which the author can infer the accuracy of the assertions. Chapter III does not examine any part of the actual procedure of candidate selection, the process whereby political parties would deliberately choose or disregard candidates because of socio-economic factors. Rather, the chapter focuses upon the end result of the process. The underlying assumption of this chapter is that this process of deciding a candidate's eligibility or ineligibility essentially occurs unconsciously or haphazardly within the political parties.

Chapters IV and V, however, do focus upon the actual selection process: both investigate the process of candidate selection from its beginning until its end. The purpose of Chapter IV is to test the effectiveness, as well as the extensiveness, of the roles of the party leadership and/or the party membership in the actual selection process. The method is to test certain assertions by Michels about the inevitability of an oligarchical party leadership; to divide arbitrarily the entire selection process into several stages; and to present statistically the candidates' perceptions—again upon the basis of the five major party groupings—of their own nomination at each stage. The examination of each stage separately permits the establishment of over-all trends about candidate selection. The theoretical basis for Chapter IV is Michels' "iron law of oligarchy," which is used as the ideal condition against which the selection process within party groupings is examined to determine how closely it approximates this ideal. This author chose Michels for two reasons. First, Michels' theory of party oligarchy is the best known. Second, Michels' theory is the most convenient and complete model yet developed of the political party. Chapter V examines the condition of the political parties as centralized or decentralized by testing the roles of various geographical levels of the party leadership in the actual process of candidate selection. The method is similar to that used in the previous chapter: the testing of certain assertions by Michels about the inevitability of party decentralization; the arbitrary division of the selection process into different stages; and the statistical presentation of the candidates' perceptions—again upon the basis of the five major party groupings—of the roles of various geographical levels of leadership in their own nominations. Michels again provides the theoretical basis: this time his theory of "localism" is used as the ideal condition against which the selection process within the party groupings is examined to determine how closely it approximates this ideal.

The third and last part of this book consists of Chapter VI, which is an assessment of the evidence and its resulting conclusions presented in this study. The author emphasizes that this study, and its consequent conclusions concerning provincial political parties, are applicable to only one Argentine province. These conclusions might perhaps be applied, with hesitation and extreme caution, to the Argentine provinces of San Juan or Tucumán. Such an application might be justified upon the basis of enough similarity in socio-economic conditions and development and/ or the political history and development of these two provinces. This author feels that these conclusions could not be applied to any other Argentine province, such as: Buenos Aires, Córdoba, Santa Fe, or the northern region of Corrientes, Formosa and Salta. One could not generalize about Argentine politics and political parties in general from the evidence presented here. One can only begin to make conclusions or assert hypotheses about politics and political parties in one certain province.

This investigation gathered information from 254 respondents, or 32% (approximately one-third) of the total number of 787 candidates nominated by these selected parties during the period 1962-1965. Of these 254 candidates 76 (30%) were chosen from the First Electoral District; 68 (27%) were chosen from the Second Electoral District; 72 (28%) were chosen from the Third Electoral District; and 38 (15%) were chosen upon a provincial-wide basis. These respondents consisted of 123 (48%) candidates for provincial deputy, 88 (35%) candidates for provincial senator, 36 (14%) candidates for national deputy and seven (3%) candidates for provincial governor. The Conservatives selected 38 (15%) of these candidates; the Radicals selected 101 (40%) of these candidates; the Peronists selected 68 (27%) of these candidates; the Socialists selected 26 (10%) of these candidates; and the Christian Democrats selected 21 (8%) of these candidates.

This study was originally presented as a doctoral dissertation. Space restrictions, however, have meant that this book has necessarily had to exclude certain portions of the original writing. Lack of sufficient space has meant the exclusion of an analysis of the socio-economic characteristics of the candidates' fathers and an analysis of certain socio-economic characteristics of the provincial population. The original dissertation should be consulted for knowledge about these aspects, together with more detailed information of the investigation. A discussion of the methodology of this investigation as well as the questionnaire used in the interviewing have been included in the Appendix.

This author acknowledges the invaluable aid and advice of Dr. Federico Gil, who decisively assisted the author to obtain the Fulbright and two Organization of American States Research Grants which enabled him to perform the necessary research in Mendoza Province. The author acknowledges the significant comments, criticisms, and suggestions made by Dr. William Keech, Dr. James Prothro, and Dr. Charles Robson. The author appreciates the invaluable help of Dr. Alberto Ciria during the analysis and presentation of this research data. This study would have been impossible without the constant and unencumbered sponsorship by Dr. Luis Campoy, director of the Institute of Sociology at the University of Cuyo, of the author during his interviewing in Mendoza Province. The author received good comments and advice in his research from Dr. José Luis de Imaz, Dr. Darío Cantón, Dr. José Enrique Miguens, Dr. Arturo Frondizi, and Félix Luna, all of Buenos Aires. The author's successful access to the Mendocino political party leaders and candidates was possible only because of his introduction and sponsorship within the individual political parties by many provincial party leaders within Mendoza Province. The author is grateful to the Memorial University of Newfoundland for financial aid in the publication of this book. Without the help of all these sources this study would have been impossible, but the author alone is responsible for the opinions, conclusions, and the theoretical bases of this work.

TABLE OF CONTENTS

THE RECRUITMENT OF CANDIDATES IN
MENDOZA PROVINCE, ARGENTINA

CHAPTER I

THE POLITICAL ENVIRONMENT OF MENDOZA PROVINCE

Mendoza Province is the principal province of the Argentine West as well as the largest and most important province of the Region of Cuyo, a geographical term indicating the three provinces of Mendoza, San Juan, and San Luis. Surrounded by the Argentine provinces of San Juan, San Luis, La Pampa, and Neuquén to the North, East, and South, Mendoza shares the Andes Mountains to the West with Chile. Mendoza is the major land port for travel and traffic to and from Chile.

The word "Cuyo" meant "sandy land" in the language of the *Araucano* Indians and refers to the condition of Mendoza Province as a semi-desert area.[1] Coming from Buenos Aires, one enters a flat plain covered by desert vegetation until arriving at the provincial capital of Mendoza from which one can see the Andes Mountains, which extend westward to Santiago, Chile. Mendoza Province is the home of the highest peak in the Western Hemisphere, Aconcagua, more than 22,000 feet. If one has traveled from El Paso, Texas, to Tucson, Arizona, one can easily imagine Mendoza Province. The province has a total of fifteen million hectares, of which 550,000 hectares (or three per cent of the land) are irrigated artificially by means of rivers from the Andes Mountains. The provincial population is concentrated in this three per cent of irrigated land.[2]

The economy of Mendoza Province is based fundamentally upon the growing of grapes and the production of derivative products. The province leads in the production of wine and the growing of grapes in Argentina. In fact, the elaboration of foods and drinks is its major industry. Mendoza Province is also an important producer of petroleum. The primary sector of the economy accounts for 32.8% of the working population and 25.1% of the gross product; the secondary sector of the economy accounts for 27.3% of the working population and 37.1% of the gross product; while the tertiary sector of the economy accounts for 28.5% of the working population and 37.8% of the gross product.[3]

The most important economic development in the history of Mendoza Province was the coming of the railroad. In 1880 construction was

---

[1] Jorge M. Scalvini, *Historia de Mendoza*, p. 53.

[2] Instituto de Investigaciones Económicas y Tecnológicas, *Esto es Mendoza*, 1965.

[3] *Ibid.* Scalvini, *Historia de Mendoza*, pp. 65-70, 243; James Scobie, *Argentina*, p. 144.

started to extend the railroad from the Province of San Luis to the Province of Mendoza. In 1885 the railroad reached the capital of Mendoza, and in 1940 a narrow gauge railroad between Mendozad and Santiago, Chile, was finished. The importance of the railroad was that it caused the development of an agro-industrial economy based upon the production of wines and other foods, as well as causing a great influx of foreign immigrants to settle the province.[4] Both these developments, in turn, influenced decisively the politics of Mendoza Province until the present moment.

In order to understand the political parties of Mendoza Province, one must understand the political environment in which these parties have operated and the conditions which have molded that environment. In Mendoza Province the norm had been the unrepresentative election, an election in which the minimum democratic conditions necessary for free expression of the popular will were absent. The systematic use of electoral violence and fraud traditionally has characterized the Argentine political culture. In Mendoza Province, as in the national scene, until 1916 the elections occurred in an atmosphere of violence and persecution of opponents by the official party, and this condition was one of the chief means by which the politico-economic Oligarchy maintained its power after the Battle of Pavón in 1861.[5] The elections of 1916 and 1918 by which the Radicals gained the national presidency and the Mendocino governorship for the first time were noteworthy for their absence of fraud in comparison to the previous experiences. The practices initiated by the former Oligarchy were continued with varying de-

[4] The term "agro-industrial economy" was suggested by Pedro R. David in his "The Social Structure of Argentina," (Ph.D. Dissertation), pp. 237-241. This thesis suggested that economics based upon the specialized production of a finished product by the processing of a raw material with a complex division of labor is the most significant feature of an "agro-industrial" society.

[5] Although there were examples of electoral violence during the elections of 1916, 1917, and 1918, these elections differed from the previous ones in the condition that the national and provincial governments seriously intended to hold honest elections, not to use force during or preceding the election, and to respect the decision of the popular will. The election of 1940 was the most honest of the period 1930 until 1943; it was free of electoral violence during the day of the election and was free of electoral trickery, except in the Department of General Alvear. However, this election was preceded by about six weeks of organized violence by the National Democratic Party, perhaps as much to curtail expression by the opposition as to create an atmosphere of fear conducive to "correct" voting. Thus, the inclusion of the election of 1940 is comparative and in no sense should be interpreted as meeting absolutely the conditions of electoral tranquility and electoral honesty.

Ezequiel Ortega's *Quiera el pueblo votar* is an investigation of the electoral conditions in Argentina from 1810 until 1912 which examines the various forms of electoral violence and trickery. In Mendoza in 1908 there were 17,000 registered voters of which 1,955 voted. See Sergio Bagú's *Evolución histórica de la estratificación social en la Argentina*, p. 67.

grees of intensity in Mendoza Province by the Lencinists, the Radical Civic Union, and the National Democratic parties during the 1920's and the 1930's. The election of 1946 was considered by all to have been singularly free of fraud and violence, and the elections since 1958 have been conducted at a high level of honesty and tolerance.[6] The condition of free press, free speech, and free assembly: that is, environment conducive to discussion and to debate of the issues and the candidates, has varied in intensity. Press censorship and curtailment of free discussion were practiced by the Peronist Government after 1948 and previously by the National Democratic and Radical Civic Union Parties.[7] Knowledge that one's vote counts or the assurance that the decision of the voters will be respected is, perhaps, the most basic characteristic of a representative election. After 1955, electoral laws existed which were designed to repress Peronism, as well as a national sense of intranquility and the insecurity of Peronist leaders that their electoral majority would be ignored. The 1962 election may be considered an exception to this situation.[8] Mendoza Province may thus be considered to have had seven representative elections throughout her political history: 1916, 1917, 1918, 1940, 1946, 1948, and 1962. But only the elections of 1918 and 1946 may be considered as being truly representative.

While internal elections within Mendocino political parties are seldom

[6] The best book illustrating the kinds of electoral violence and fraud used specifically in Mendoza Province is by R. R. Gil, *El ex concejal Juan Puebla*, the political autobiography of a young leader of the Democratic Party who was elected municipal councilman for the Department of Maipú in 1941. See also Oscar Maidana Díaz, *Dinastía de los Lencinas; Los Andes*, August and September, 1930; 27 July 1931, p. 5; 25 November 1940, p. 6; 28 November 1940, p. 5; 4 January 1941, p. 7; Nicolás Repetto, *Mi paso por la política*, pp. 297-299; Lucas Ayarragaray, *Cuestiones y problemas argentinos contemporáneos*, II, pp. 182-186.

[7] The individual use of organized violence by Democratic Party members and by the provincial police or armed groups had the effect of prohibiting the freedom of speech and assembly. During the 1928-1930 Intervention in Mendoza Province the Radical Civic Union burned all copies of the newspapers unfavorable to its government. See *Los Andes*, 7 September 1930, p. 3.

[8] In 1955 the Peronist Party was dissolved by presidential decree. In November of 1958 the Frondizi Government passed a law which dissolved the party and declared it to be illegal. Also the government prohibited the Peronists, under other party names, to nominate their own candidates. However, before the 1962 election Frondizi announced that the Peronists could nominate their own candidates for all public office and could campaign freely, but under the names of other parties, as the Peronist name was still illegal.

Frondizi indicated that he intended to respect the outcome of the election. The Peronists won control of the major provinces. The Peronists' victory caused the army to revolt, to overthrow the government, and to annul the electoral victory of the Peronists. After the Revolt of 1962 the Peronists were again severely restricted in electoral participations. Undoubtedly, the Revolt of 1962 only increased the insecurity of the Peronists in fear that their electoral victories would not be respected.

characterized by the use of electoral violence, they are considered to be characterized by electoral fraud. The main type of fraud is the use of double registers of the membership. Illegally, persons are registered in two or three different political parties. The purpose is to allow members of particular parties to vote and to decide candidacies in internal elections of opposing political parties. The double registers are often used by political leaders to win elections by garnering the votes of relatives or close friends, even though publically known to be aligned with another political party. Another method is not to allow the opposition faction to obtain new membership registers for use in the election or not to allow the opposing faction to purify the registers by removing persons since dead, moved away, or registered in other parties. Other methods are the sudden convocation of meetings and the authoritarian conduct of meetings.[9]

In Argentina the "political rules of the game" are based upon conformity and intransigence, in contrast to the dissent and compromise accepted and promoted by the institutions and traditions of the Anglo-American political systems. In Argentine political parties the dissenter is not viewed as a social critic but rather is viewed as a personal enemy, while the compromiser is viewed as a weakling who has become less *macho*.[10] One characteristic of the political-institutional life of Argentina is that those advocating a representative democracy deny the possibility of a minimum dissension necessary for the functioning of a pluralistic society. One explanation of a multi-party system in Argentina is the absence of an internal pluralism within the political parties. Political leaders develop an emotional *Weltschaunung* based upon extreme moral and ethical grounds which does not permit opposition or criticism, within or without the party.[11] The typical cycle of Argentine politics is the following: the rejection of the political opposition causes its alienation; just before the rupture of the political system, acceptance is granted to the new elements in society represented by the opposition; this acceptance causes the opposition's victory; the victorious opposition now acts like

[9] These situations of internal fraud are characteristic of the lower levels of the party organization: at the municipal level or lower sectional level. Party leaders consider that at the provincial level, there exists a high degree of honesty.

[10] The word "macho" refers to the vigorous demonstration of one's masculinity: in the political scale of values, a demonstration of courage and bravery. The ideal of the Argentine politician, and the expectation of his followers, is that he will be valiant. Rosas, Yrigoyen, and Perón were considered as valiant by the popular classes. See Mafud, *El desarraigo argentino*, p. 65.

[11] See Richard W. Weatherhead, "The Forces of Change and Continuity," in Joseph Maier and Richard Weatherhead, *Politics of Change in Latin America*, pp. 37-41; L. Campoy, *Factors That Led to the Successful Revolt of 1930 and the Revolution of 1943 in Argentina*, pp. 60-65; Silvia Sigal and Ezequiel Gallo, "La formación de los partidos contemporáneos: La Unión Cívica Radical (1890-1916)," *Desarrollo Económico*, III (1963), p. 183; J. Mafud, *El desarraigo . . .*, pp. 65-68.

its political predecessors. This condition of conformity and intransigence and its subsequent effects is considered characteristic of the Radical Civic Union.[12]

The pragmatic political realism of the North American type is absent from the Argentine political culture. In North America the political realism is based upon a store of political knowledge, a knowledge formed by reason and common sense speculating upon past experience and present empirical evidence. Such an outlook is alien to the Argentine experience with three consequent results. One result is that the Constitution and other formal political regulations are idealistic expressions of the desires and the intentions. Political institutions are viewed in terms of how they ought to be, instead of being seen in terms of how they can or will be. Thus, when the Constitution or a political institution inevitably breaks down, the difficulty is considered solved by reforming a constitutional clause or by regulating a political institution more idealistically. Any feeling or pressure to reform or to revolutionize the institution is absent. Another result is the desire to imitate the foreign experiences and institutions as the best solution to Argentina's problems and situations, and the tendency to deprecate—if not to reject outrightly —Argentina's own natural institutions and experiences as inferior. In effect, the Argentine has always conceived of Argentina upon the basis of the European experience, rather than of conceiving Europe upon the basis of the Argentine experience.[13] A third result is the existence of a "scapegoat" as the explanation of political history. Every government or political party explains its difficulties or failures as the fault or the error of some outside cause or conspiracy. Originally, the Indian served as the scapegoat; after his disappearance he was replaced by the gaucho. When these explanations disappeared as obvious and acceptable reasons, then the tradition began of selecting the opposing political party or government as the scapegoat.[14]

Mafud contends that this absense of compromise makes the political parties act as disintegrative forces in a society in which all sectors of society do not share common political and ideological goals. This socio-ideological division of society and this disintegrative effect of the multi-party system re-inforce each other. Mafud, *Psicología de la viveza criolla*, pp. 334-337; Eduardo Laurencena, *Centralismo y federalismo*, pp. 110-111.

[12] Darío Cantón, "Argentine Parliamentarians 1889, 1916, 1946," (M.A. Thesis), p. 123. Alberto Ciria, *Partidos y poder en la Argentina moderna (1930-1946)*, p. 148.

[13] José Ingenieros, "La anarquía argentina y el caudillismo," in *Sociología argentina*, p. 115; Campoy, *Factors That Led . . .*, pp. 60-65; Mafud, *El desarraigo . . .*, pp. 109-164. One of the criticisms of the Argentine Socialist Party is that its principles and programs tend to be based upon the European experience rather than upon the Argentine conditions. See Eduardo Laurencena, *Centralismo y federalismo*, pp. 111-112.

[14] Mafud, *El desarraigo . . .*, pp. 68-70.

One difference between the English political experience and the Argentine political experience has been that in England the total political mobilization of all sectors of society occurred concurrently with the political integration of all sectors of society. In the English experience the development of a representative democracy, in which each sector of the population was successively mobilized until the total population was included, was preceded by and accompanied simultaneously by the creation of a basic ideological consensus among all groups, and with the development of mechanisms of social and political integration. These mechanisms effectively absorbed each successively mobilized sector of society by assuring its political participation upon the basis of certain shared norms. In effect, political pluralism developed simultaneously with political and ideological unity. Argentina, however, has failed to develop such mechanisms of integration, although all sectors of the population have been mobilized for political participation. One major cause of this absence of consensus and integration was the entrance into Argentina of a great mass of immigrants in a very brief period of years at a time when the Argentine society lacked the cultural and social institutions sufficiently strong enough to receive and to assimilate this immigrant mass and still maintain its social equilibrium. This sudden impact of immigrants destroyed the native social structure and native national character of creole Argentina simultaneously as the cultural institutions of the immigrants were destroyed in the process of moving. Concurrently, the Argentine has not yet been able to develop his own social personality for lack of sufficient time plus the fact that his world is changing continuously and rapidly. Thus, the Argentine is rootless in an atmosphere of competing cultures, differing mental attitudes, and unconnected social statuses.[15]

This rootlessness has several significant effects in the political style practiced by the Argentine. It may explain the particular political instability of the last 30 years. It produces an individual who is completely egotistical. The Argentine exalts and exaggerates his individuality and acts upon the basis of his own personal benefit, not benefit for the common good. Yet, while the individual Argentine may act upon the basis of a Machiavellian personality, in which is absent the communal spirit and its resulting social attachments,[16] the Argentine is critical of this same quality in his politicians. Thus, there exists an unfavorable concept of the politician. Public opinion characterizes Argentine politicians as the beneficiaries of secret investments, bribes, and sinecures;

[15] Gino Germani, *Política y sociedad en una época de transición,* pp. 154-162, 200, 209-210; Julio Mafud, *El desarraigo . . .,* pp. 80-93, 136-37.

[16] Mafud, pp. 136-137; Germani, p. 210. The term "Machiavellian personality" was suggested to the author by an unknown Argentine psychologist at a cocktail party.

as persons who need to lie by promising everything and completing nothing, who act for personal and ulterior motives instead of disinterested service. Politics is seen as the occupation of the professionals, the audacious, or the amoral persons—in which the honorable persons refuse to participate.[17] Complementary to depreciation of the politician is a depreciation of the democratic system and of democratic institutions. The common attitude is that democracy is a failure in Argentina and that the present socio-economic troubles are caused by a dysfunctional democratic system of parties and elections.[18]

The other effect of this rootlessness is the cult of friendship and of personal allegiance, which serves as a factor of cohesion and social integration. The individual finds his security in the man: his protector, his employer, and his political leaders. The individual does not find his safeguards in his society nor in its Constitution and laws.[19] This emphasis upon the personal relationship in politics explains the *caudillo* and the system of *caudillismo,* which means the exercise of personal political authority independent of any representation of collective interests within the society. The basis of the caudillo is the personal relationship developed upon sympathy and not rationality: the relationship of the leader or conductor as well as the sympathetic-personal relationship. Also, the caudillos developed to represent the popular concept and desire for justice and always lead the social protest which caused them. The caudillo is a political activist who congregates a nucleus of supporters-followers by functioning as an "errand boy" for his followers.[20]

[17] Ramón Gil, *El ex concejal . . .,* pp. 14, 23, 88, 113, 120, 136, 148; José Luis de Imaz, *Los que mandan,* pp. 206.

[18] Ingenieros, "La anarquía . . .," p. 124; Gil, *El ex concejal . . .,* p. 114. The use of fraud during the 1930's to frustrate the electoral decision of the popular classes created an attitude of profound scepticism of the democratic system. Simultaneously, there occurred a massive immigration of the population from the Interior Provinces to Buenos Aires, who did not find the institutional means necessary to express their desires or to integrate themselves into the democratic system. This situation explains that in Argentina the totalitarian movement of Peronism was to give the popular classes their first really direct intervention in political decision making. Gino Germani, *Política y sociedad . . .,* pp. 229-231, 252. A similar attitude is expressed by Walter Beveraggi Allende in his *El fracaso de Perón y el problema argentino,* p. 27.

[19] Likewise the political system is seen as depending upon the right man instead of upon the principles and institutions of the system. The common attitude among politicians is that every political party depends upon the appearance of the great national leader at the right moment. Every movement needs the conductor who incarnates the principles, doctrine, and ideals of the party as well as guiding and representing the movement by his simple presence. It is illusionary to conceive of the political party as motivated by principles or policies. See Ignacio Covarrubias, "El 'misterio' de Don Gilberto Suárez Lago," *Leoplán,* 26 (1960), p. 21. See also Mafud, *Psicología de . . .,* pp. 96-99; José Ingenieros, "La anarquía . . .," p. 119.

[20] R. A. Gómez, "Argentine Federalism," (Ph.D. Thesis), pp. 146-147; Dardo Olguín, *Lencinas,* pp. 10-11. In the opinion of the author, one of the best portraits

The result is that the political parties are structured around this system of caudillos in the form of a pyramid in which the provincial caudillo occupies the apex, various classes of caudillos occupy the intermediate and lower levels, until finally at the very bottom of the pyramid is located the party membership. This membership is divided into groups, each group of which is aggregated around a certain caudillo of the town or of the ward who is called a "sargento" caudillo because he deals directly with the voters. The *"coronel"* caudillos generally are the department leaders, who act as middle-men between the provincial "general" and the municipal "sargento."[21] This pyramidal structure embodies relationships of power and obligations upward and downward within all levels of party leaders. The power of the provincial caudillo is in direct proportion to his ability to maintain the loyalty and the support of these lower caudillos, and likewise any candidacy is the result of an aggregation of local caudillos.[22] Traditionally, the party membership has been represented by means of decisions made among its caudillos and not by direct participation of the membership itself.

This concept of the pyramidal structure of the political parties is often applied to the governmental system as well. While Argentina may have a federal system in theory, all students of the Argentine feel that it is not a federal system in practice. Institutionally, they feel that Argentina has been transformed from a federal into a unitary state.[23] The main cause for this transformation has been the president's intervention power. Under this power the president may intervene in any

---

in English of the contemporary Argentine caudillo would be William L. Riorden's *Plunkett of Tammany Hall.* A good, but brief, assessment of the Argentine caudillo is in José L. Romero, *A History of Argentine Political Thought,* pp. 109-112.

[21] This structural analysis and terminology represent an idealized model. For example, the Democratic Party would probably be best characterized as having a collegial leadership of provincial caudillos, while the Radical and Peronist parties would tend to a leadership by one maximum leader, or, at best, two. Structurally, all parties have a provincial committee (council, commission, or directive committee) consisting of constitutionally named officials and departmental representatives. Each department consists of a similar organization, while the youth and women's movements have their own parallel levels of leadership. Besides these officials, each party has a provincial congress, which usually meets once a year, and constitutionally is the most authoritative party organ to decide party policy and party candidacies, if the candidacies are not decided by an internal election. Only the Democratic Party uses the system of District Congresses to decide party candidacies.

[22] The influence of the caudillos is decreased by the effective opposition of another internal party faction. The Radical parties are considered the most traditional in still basing their structure upon the caudillo. See Campobassi and others, *Los partidos políticos: estructura y vigencia en la Argentina,* pp. 47-48.

[23] Zorraquín Becú, *El federalismo Argentino,* pp. 270-272; George Blanksten, *Perón's Argentina,* p. 146; R. A. Gómez, "Argentine Federalism," p. 260; Alfredo Vítolo, "Intervencionismo del estado," *Cuadernos de Proceso,* I (1952), p. 26.

province (generally at his discretion), remove its provincial authorities, and appoint his own representative as interim governor.[24] The president's power to declare a state of siege, the national government's control of the tax resources, broad interpretation of its Constitutional powers by the national government, the tradition of a strong national executive, and the socio-economic centralization of Buenos Aires over the Interior Provinces all reinforce and encourage the unitary system despite the use of staggered elections and the presidential form of government. Students of the Argentine consider that independent provinces with their own political autonomy and their own cultural peculiarities have become suffocated by a double centralization: political, economic, and cultural centralization in Buenos Aires; and provincial governments which must march in unison with the national government and which are completely monopolized by the national government by means of its constitutional and legal powers. This national centralization means that the national president's power is unchecked and that the provincial governors have become the electoral and administrative agents of the president. The common view is that a national centralization within the political parties parallels this national centralization within the government. In Argentine parties, activity is seen as coming from the top down, and national legislative and provincial gubernatorial candidates are considered to be selected without decisive provincial participation.[25]

Perhaps this national centralization was necessary because Argentina is divided into two distinct and contrasting regions: the area of Buenos Aires and the area of the Interior Provinces. The Province of Buenos Aires and the Federal Capital were to experience an economic, social, and spiritual development distinct from that of the Interior Provinces. The Interior Provinces were settled by colonists from Perú and Chile; they developed historically according to the traditional Spanish values and characteristics, which rejected the political values of the French Revolution, which sought to reaffirm the native values, and which emphasized the dominant role of the Church. The Interior Provinces developed a more rigid social system and were concerned to protect their native home industries. The Province of Buenos Aires rejected these values and characteristics of the Interior Provinces because it was settled directly from Europe and looked to the French Revolution as the source of its liberal political values. Buenos Aires became oriented towards Europe because of its development as a trading center based upon a great commercial traffic with Europe. The residents of the Interior

[24] Zorraquín Becú, *El federalismo* . . ., pp. 248-249; Matienzo, *El gobierno representativo,* pp. 200, 231-233; Gómez, "Argentine Federalism," pp. 186, 193-206.

[25] L. S. Rowe, *The Federal System of the Argentine Republic,* pp. 4-10, 81; Gómez, "Argentine Federalism," pp. 151, 157-158, 228, 252-260; Zorraquín Becú, *El federalismo* . . ., pp. 272-274; Bagú, *Evolución histórica de* . . ., pp. 66-67; Vítolo, *Cuadernos de Proceso,* I (1952), p. 26.

Provinces are known as *provincianos* who dislike and suspect Buenos Aires and its inhabitants, known as *porteños*. The Interior Provinces feel that Buenos Aires developed and progressed at the expense of the Interior Provinces, which are not understood and represented by the Province of Buenos Aires.[26]

Within this situation Mendoza Province occupies a special position. The impact of European influences in the Interior Provinces is limited to the Provinces of Tucumán and Mendoza. Roads, schools, hospitals, and even politics have always had more attention in Mendoza Province than in any other Interior Province.[27] The Region of Cuyo was originally settled by immigrants from Chile, whereas the rest of Argentina was originally settled by immigrants coming directly from Perú or Spain. These factors explain why Mendoza Province has a strong sense of regionalism and a special pride. Within political party development Mendoza Province has always had a strong sense of independence and provincial autonomy, as exemplified by the experiences of the provincial Radical Civic Union and by Tres Banderas within the Peronist Movement.[28]

This centralization of the provinces under the direction of Buenos Aires-Federal Capital is paralleled by a similar centralization within each province. The socio-economic-political life of each province is centralized in the provincial capital. This provincial centralization is maintained and protected by the national centralization. Within the province the governor is considered by students of the Argentine to be more power-

[26] This divergence between Buenos Aires and the Interior Provinces is reflected in its political aspect by the fact that the Neo-Peronist movement has developed only in the Interior; it has not developed in the Province of Buenos Aires. One Conservative leader from Mendoza charged that the failure of the entire Conservative movement in Argentina would be due to the inability to develop a common national party program since the bifurcation between the Province of Buenos Aires and the remainder of the country would not permit the transcendency of political ideas and actions formulated in the interior of the nation. See *Los Andes,* 27 June 1966, p. 9; Máximo Etchecopar, *Esquema de la Argentina*, pp. 141-151; James R. Scobie, *Argentina*, pp. 136-137; Juan Lazarte, *Federalismo y descentralización en la cultura Argentina*, pp. 218-234; Ernesto Palacio, *Historia de Argentina*, I, pp. 86-136; Blanksten, *Perón's Argentina*, pp. 17-19, 134.

[27] Scobie, *Argentina*, pp. 145, 149; Rowe, *The Federal System* . . ., pp. 3-4.

[28] Mendocinos regard themselves as living in a province distinct from the other provinces of Argentina. The common opinion is that Mendoza Province is more progressive than any other province, with a higher standard of living, with much more economic and commercial activity, but avoiding the banes of the big industrial and commercial center of Buenos Aires.

Mendoza Province is particular in that it is one of the strongholds of the Democratic Party, but has a higher rate of literacy, higher per capita income, a larger middle class based upon a system of small landowners, and a higher ratio of urban settlement than the Provinces of San Luis and Corrientes—the other Democratic Provinces. Mendocino Democrats consider themselves as directing the national Conservative movement, rather than being directed by it.

ful than a North American governor and to be decisive in the selection of legislative candidates. Scholars of the Argentine generally have agreed that the principle of the separation of powers, characteristic of the presidential form of government, had been replaced by a fusion of powers at the provincial as well as at the national level. Scholars consider that, in reality, the executive power is unchecked and not balanced effectively by an independent legislative or judicial power. The judiciary always depends directly or indirectly upon the executive, while the political party system makes the provincial governor control the legislature. The common view is that Argentina has inherited and has maintained the Spanish tradition of a strong executive dominating the entire institutional system.[29]

In Mendoza Province both the governor and the vice-governor must be native Argentines (or sons of native Argentines), thirty years old, and for five years continuously a resident of that province. Previously, the provincial constitutions had required the provincial governor to meet additional requirements such as being: a native of the province, a person thirty-five years old, a member of the Roman Catholic Church, an owner of property. Both the governor and the vice-governor serve a three-year term and neither may be re-elected immediately to either position. Previously, the Constitutions of 1894 and 1949 provided for a four year term of office. Originally, the gubernatorial officials were elected by an electoral college composed of the provincial legislators plus an equal number of popularly chosen electors. The Constitution of 1916 provided that the governor should be elected directly, and this system was used in Mendoza Province until 1963. After the Army Revolt of 1962 the Guido Government decreed that the gubernatorial officials were to be elected in 1963 in all Argentine provinces by an Electoral College, chosen in the provincial election upon the basis of the D'Hont System of Proportional Representation. The provincial legislature was to decide if the Electoral College failed.[30] In the election of 1966 it was intended that the new governor and vice-governor would be directly elected under the system started in 1916. However, the preceding year the provincial leaders of the Democratic Party and Popular Radical Civic Union made

[29] Lazarte, *Federalismo y descentralización* . . ., pp. 105-106. Gómez, "Argentine Federalism," pp. 105, 142, 177; Lazarte, *Federalismo y descentralización* . . ., p. 160; Matienzo, *El gobierno representativo*, pp. 185-186; Rowe, *The Federal System* . . ., pp. 95-99; Galletti, *La política y los partidos*, pp. 229.

[30] Carlos R. Melo, "Las constituciones de la provincia de Mendoza," *Boletín de la Facultad de Derecho y Ciencias Sociales de la Universidad Nacional de Córdoba*, 27 (1963), pp. 9-162; Scalvini, *Historia de* . . ., p. 282; Melo, *Los Partidos* . . ., pp. 111-112; *Los Andes*, 17 June 1965, p. 1; *Constitución de la provincia de Mendoza (1963)*, pp. 33-36. The Constitution of 1916, which provided for the popular and direct election of the governor, was written by a provincial constitutional convention in which the Socialists were the largest minority. See Olguín, *Lencinas*, p. 208.

a verbal agreement, that the provincial Constitutional Convention convoked in 1965 would award itself the power to amend the provincial constitution to continue the system used in 1963. The leaders further agreed that both parties would vote for whichever party's candidates received the highest number of votes. The purpose of the agreement was to prevent the election of the Peronists' candidate to the governorship by the direct popular vote, almost assured upon the basis of the voting statistics from the election of 1965.

After 1894 Mendoza Province replaced its unicameral legislature by the bicameral system of the Chamber of Deputies and the Chamber of Senators. The provincial deputy must be 21 years old, an Argentine citizen, and two years resident in Mendoza Province. The provincial senator must be thirty years old. From 1894 until 1965, with the exception of the Perón Government, the deputy served a three year term of office and could be re-elected, while the senator served a six year term of office and also was re-eligible. In 1965 the provincial constitution was amended to provide for a four year term of office for both groups of legislators—the same system used during the Perón Government. The elections of provincial legislators are staggered: annually one-third of the provincial deputies are elected and biannually one-third of the provincial senators are elected. The national government has always had a bicameral legislature of the Chamber of Deputies and the Chamber of Senators. The national deputy must be twenty-five years old, an Argentine citizen, and two years a resident of the province. The national senator must be thirty years old, an Argentine citizen, two years a resident of the province, and have a certain annual income.[31] The deputy serves a four year term and the senator, nine years; both are re-eligible for election. The deputies are elected by popular vote in each province upon the basis of population, and Mendoza Province elects seven deputies. The two senators from each province have always been elected by the provincial legislature, except during the Perón Government when the senators were directly chosen by popular election. The elections of the national legislators are staggered: one third of the 34 senators are chosen every three years, while one-half of the 186 deputies are elected every two years.[32] Provincial, as well as national, legislative sessions are annual and begin in May and end in November.

[31] Since 1853 the national legislators have received a regular yearly salary. It was not until 1920, under the initiative of José N. Lencinas, that the system of salaries for the provincial legislators was started in the Province of Mendoza. Julio Fernández-Peláez, *Historia de Maipú*, p. 142.

[32] *Constitución de la provincia de Mendoza (1963)*, pp. 20-23; Mario Alexandre, *Instrucción cívica*, pp. 225-238; Melo, *Boletín de la Facultad de Derechos y Ciencias Sociales de la Universidad Nacional de Córdoba*, 27 (1963), pp. 9-162; *Constitución de la provincia de Mendoza (1949)*, pp. 38-43; *Los Andes*, 4 December 1965, p. 5.

Originally, national deputies were elected by a plurality vote, either by the system of the complete list for the entire province or the system of one deputy for each electoral district within the province. Mendoza Province used the system of proportional representation for provincial deputies combined with a system of plurality vote for provincial senators. From 1912 until 1962 the electoral system, both nationally and provincially, was the incomplete list system created by the Sáenz Peña Law.[33] Under this system each party presented its list of candidates for only two-thirds of the legislative vacancies. The party winning the highest plurality of votes elected two-thirds, or a majority, of the legislators. The party winning the second highest number of votes elected one-third, or a minority, of the legislators. After the Army Revolt of 1962 the Guido Government decreed that both national deputies and provincial legislators were to be elected by the D'Hont System of Proportional Representation for the election of 1963. This system has been retained for the succeeding elections.[34] At present, the legislative candidate's position on the ballot is electorally decisive. In the election of provincial legislators and municipal officials the voter always has had to vote the entire list without the right to strike out names or to substitute other candidates. However, until the election of 1963 the voter could strike out names or substitute names of candidates of other parties in the election of national deputies. In 1962 the Guido Government decreed the replacement of cross-list voting by straight list voting in the election of national deputies. At present, while the voter must vote the straight list for the candidates of a certain office, the voter is free to practice cross-ballot voting in the selection of candidates for different offices.[35]

[33] Ministerio de Gobierno, *Registro oficial de Mendoza,* I (1895), p. 598; Scalvini, *Historia . . .,* p. 378; Alexandre, *Instrucción . . .,* pp. 127-243; Ministerio de Interior, *Régimen electoral (15 December 1959),* p. 23; Ministerio de Gobierno, *Régimen electoral de la provincia (1960),* pp. 33-34. During the Perón Government the legislators were elected according to the original system: one national deputy was elected from each electoral constituency into which Mendoza Province was divided; the provincial senators were elected from each department of the province; and the provincial deputies were elected according to the system of the incomplete list for the entire province.

[34] Ministerio de Gobierno, *Régimen electoral de la provincia (1965),* pp. 33-34; Alexandre, *Instrucción . . .,* pp. 127-143; Melo, *Los partidos . . .,* pp. 111-112. A common joke among Peronist politicians is that Illia and his Radical government, the Popular Radical Civic Union, continued the system of proportional representation after 1963 as a part of their national campaign of alphabetization. Under this system of proportional representation the Argentine politicians would have to learn rapidly the simple arithmetic of addition, subtraction, multiplications, and division in order to know if they had been elected or not.

[35] Ministerio del Interior, *Régimen electoral nacional (Mayo 1963),* pp. 22-27; Ministerio de Gobierno, *Régimen electoral de la provincia (1960),* p. 34. At present, candidates are declared elected accordingly as they lead on the list. Candi-

Mendoza Province has always used the system of multi-member legislative constituencies, with variations or in combination with single member constituencies. For the election of the province's national deputies Mendoza Province serves as one multi-member constituency. In the 1894 Constitution the province was divided into three electoral districts for the election of provincial deputies, while senators were elected by this system of districts after 1916. These electoral districts have generally maintained the same geographic divisions since then, with the addition or subtraction of a department to reflect population changes. From the election of 1958 until the election of 1965 the province was divided into three constituencies, each of which elected twelve provincial deputies and nine provincial senators.[36] In the 1965 provincial Constitutional Convention the Third Electoral District was divided into two separate electoral districts and each of the four constituencies was assigned varying numbers of legislators according to its population. The change was supported by the Radical, Democratic, and Peronist leaders.

dates which follow in order are declared to be supplements and replace vacant legislative positions according to the list's order until the next election.

36. Ministerio de Gobierno, *Registro oficial de Mendoza (1895)*, I, p. 583; Ministerio de Gobierno, *Régimen electoral de la provincia (1960)*, p. 38.

CHAPTER II

A HISTORY OF MENDOCINO POLITICAL PARTIES

Mendoza Province historically has always enjoyed a peculiar kinship with Chile: first, Mendoza was originally settled by Spanish Conquistadors who crossed over the Andes from Chile; second, the province and its capital city were named in honor of García Hurtado de Mendoza, who was appointed governor of Chile in 1557. Three years later this governor authorized Captain Pedro del Castillo to conquer the region of Cuyo. On March 2, 1561, Captain Pedro del Castillo built a fort to indicate officially a new city, which he named Mendoza in honor of the Governor of Chile.[1] Until 1776 the Province of Cuyo formed part of the General Captaincy of Chile. In that year the Province of Cuyo was added to the Viceroyalty of the Río de la Plata because the region's commercial connections were with Tucumán and Buenos Aires rather than with Chile, and because the inhabitants felt ignored and subordinated by the colonial government located in Chile.

The first period in the political history of Mendoza Province began during the War of Independence against Spain. General San Martín used Mendoza as his base for the preparation and equipment of his Army of the Andes from 1815-1817—which is considered responsible for the liberation from Spain of Chile and Perú, as well as of Argentina. During the years 1820 until 1862, Argentina and Mendoza were the scenes of civil wars between the Unitarians and the Federalists over the question of which fundamental principles were to be the basis of the new Argentine nation. The Unitarians advocated the formation of a nationally centralized state under the leadership of the Province of Buenos Aires. The Federalists advocated the formation of a federation under the leadership of the Interior Provinces.[2] Until 1852 Mendoza was

[1] Jorge M. Scalvini, *Historia de Mendoza*, pp. 34-49. Mendocino historians dispute whether the true founder of Mendoza is Pedro del Castillo or Juan Júfre. On March 28, 1562, Juan Jufré founded the present city of Mendoza, which he called Resurrection after he intentionally bypassed the fort constructed by Pedro del Castillo to mark the site of the city which del Castillo had named Mendoza in 1561.

[2] The basic ideological dispute between the Unitarians and the Federalists concerned how the new Argentine nation was to be organized. The Unitarians conceived of the new nation as a continuation of the former Spanish Viceroyalty, in which the national government and its institutions had existed before the provinces and thus, were superior to the provinces. The Federalists argued that the provinces had existed before the nation, which had been formed as an aggregation of independent provinces. Thus, the nation was based upon a federal compact in

Federalist in spirit and action. While a Unitarian sentiment existed in Mendoza and while many members of the creole ruling class were Unitarians, they were ineffective in determining provincial policy. For example, the traditional system of the town council (Cabildo Abierto) was replaced by a popularly elected Council of Representatives (Sala de Representantes) because the town council was managed by the Unitarians. In 1831 Mendoza joined the Confederation of Argentina, formed under the leadership of Juan Manuel de Rosas. This decision stemmed from the Battle of Rodeo del Chacón in Mendoza on March 28, 1831, between troops under Videla Castillo (Unitarian Governor of Mendoza) and the troops of Facundo Quiroga, Federalist ally of Rosas. The battle determined that the region of Cuyo was to be included within the Federalist system. After this battle most of the Mendocino Unitarians went into voluntary exile in Chile. Even under the commonly called Dictatorship of Rosas, Mendoza actually enjoyed a condition of autonomy.[3]

In 1861 at the Battle of Pavón the Army of the Province of Buenos Aires under the command of Bartolomé Mitre defeated the Army of the Interior Provinces under the command of Justo José de Urquiza. The significance of the Battle of Pavón is that it marks the end of government and leadership by the Federalists and the beginning of government and leadership by the Unitarians. In effect, the Battle of Pavón decided that the politico-economic institutions of contemporary Argentina, as well as of Mendoza, were to be structured upon the Unitarians' principles. The Battle of Pavón signified that Mendoza, like Argentina, was to be developed and governed politically by a minority of certain interest groups who soon formed the Oligarchy guided by their own selfish interests.[4]

The first of the modern Argentine political parties, the Radical Civic Union, was founded on June 26, 1891. It stemmed from a division in the National Committee of the Civic Union (a political movement initiated the preceding year) between Radicals who favored electoral pacts

---

which the provincial government and the provincial institutions were at least equal with, if not superior to, the national government. This public debate about the political organization of Argentina in reality was caused by a fundamental conflict between the Province of Buenos Aires and the Interior Provinces in economic orientation, a matter never publically debated. The economic health and interest of the Province of Buenos Aires depended upon an extensive foreign trade, while the economic health and interest of the Interior Provinces depended upon the protection of their native home industries against foreign imports.

Miron Burgin's *Aspectos económicos del federalismo Argentino,* p. 19. José Luis Romero's *A History of Argentine Political Thought,* pp. 61-125, contains the best discussion of the Unitarian-Federalist political ideas. Burgin's book specifically examines the economic basis of the Unitarian-Federalist dispute.

[3] Scalvini, *Historia de Mendoza,* pp. 161-247.

[4] Scalvini, *Historia de Mendoza,* pp. 107-108, 246, 273, and 285.

and political cooperation with opposing political parties, known as "acuer-distas" or later "unionists," and Radicals who opposed such electoral pacts and political co-operation, known as "intransigents." This internal division was to characterize the Radical Civic Union until the present day. The major leader of the intransigents was Alem, and after his suicide in 1896, Hipólito Yrigoyen.[5]

On December 30, 1891, Leandro Alem visited Mendoza Province and met José Nestor Lencinas. In this meeting Alem and J. N. Lencinas agreed that Lencinas was to organize the Radical Civic Union Party in Mendoza.[6] From the beginning of his activity as Radical leader until his death in 1920, as the first Radical governor of Mendoza, J. N. Lencinas was continuously in conflict with opposition elements within his own party or in conflict with the provincial or national government. Unable to participate in honest or fair elections as the means to gain control of the national and provincial governments legally, the Radical Civic Union resorted to the policy of seizing the government illegally by means of revolution or adhering to the policy of electoral abstention and total refusal to participate and to co-operate with the oligarchical governments. In 1905 the Radical Party attempted to seize the government by revolution. While this Revolution failed in the rest of Argentina, it was successful in Mendoza. J. N. Lencinas assumed the provincial governorship for some days until overthrown by the advance of national troops sent from Buenos Aires.[7] Within the party Lencinas was constantly opposed by Pedro N. Ortiz over questions of the party's candidates, as in the elections of 1914 and 1916, or over the policy of the electoral participation in the provincial elections.

The second period in the political history of Mendoza started with the election of J. N. Lencinas in 1918 as governor of Mendoza. The election of 1918 marked the beginning of thirteen years of Radical provincial governments as well as the formation of the Conservative Party, forerunner of the present-day Democratic Party of Mendoza. The governorship of Lencinas is memorable in three respects. First, Lencinas initiated the first labor laws in Argentina, limiting the hours of labor, requiring the minimum wage, and creating old-age and accident pensions. Second, Lencinas initiated a social revolution in Mendoza by assuring the participation of the "common man" in the provincial government. For the first time union leaders, immigrants, and long time party hacks and departmental caudillos occupied government positions in fulfillment of the populist concept that any man can govern. Lencinas was

[5] Gabriel del Mazo, *El radicalismo*, I, pp. 71, 93-97, 207. The best history of the Radical Party is the three volume study, in Spanish, by del Mazo. The only study in English is Peter Snow's *Argentine Radicalism*.

[6] Dardo Olguín, *Lencinas*, pp. 31, 72-84.

[7] *Ibid.*, pp. 163, 180, 192-206, 368 and 369.

a provincial caudillo who represented the middle and lower classes, until then politically inexperienced social sectors which had been systematically excluded from political participation by the provincial Oligarchy formed after the Battle of Pavón.[8]

Third, Lencinas, as governor, increasingly clashed with the national Radical president, Yrigoyen. Three basic differences between Lencinas and Yrigoyen caused these disputes, which—when carried to their logical conclusions—resulted in the formation of an independent Radical party in Mendoza led by Lencinas' son, Carlos Washington Lencinas, and the bulk of Lencinas supporters. One basic difference between Lencinas and Yrigoyen was in their political outlook. Essentially, Yrigoyen was an evolutionist, who sought moderate change and who was scrupulous and legalistic in his political methods. He was willing to allow the Oligarchy to exist alongside of the Radical Civic Union. Essentially, Lencinas was a revolutionist, who desired to alter fundamentally the system and to crush completely the old Oligarchy. Lencinas accepted violence as a political weapon normal to the Interior Provinces. The second basic difference between Lencinas and Yrigoyen was over the sphere of influence assigned to each. Yrigoyen firmly believed that the success of Radicalism in Mendoza Province was caused solely by his efforts and success as president. Also, Yrigoyen wished to extend his hegemony over the Interior Provinces within the Radical Party and to assure the selection, as governors, of persons amenable to his central control and personal direction. Lencinas, in contrast, was concerned to maintain complete independence within his province. Lencinas considered himself autonomous within the sphere of his own province. The third basic difference lay in their personalities. Lencinas was closer in personality to Alem, the passionate idealist, than to Yrigoyen, who appeared a cold, calculating realist in contrast. Lencinas was a passionate leader of a sentimentally popular movement and the expression of the profound provincial regionalism of Mendoza.[9]

Yrigoyen attempted to solve these conflicts by intervention in Mendoza Province. In 1919 Yrigoyen intervened in order to solve an internal party dispute between younger party leaders led by Lencinas and the older party leaders led by the Vice-Governor Delfín Alvarez. Upon the death of Lencinas in 1920, Yrigoyen intervened in an attempt to assure the selection of Rufino Ortega as gubernatorial candidate in the

[8] Olguín, *Lencinas*, pp. 302-303; *Dos políticos y dos políticas*, pp. 94, 108-109, 141; Benito Marianetti, *Argentina: realidad y perspectiva*, p. 343. The popular concept of the Radical Civic Union Party (until the advent of Perón) was that it was the political party of the "common man," consisting of politicians who lacked the necessary technical experience for governmental positions. One newspaper referred to this period of Radical government as the triumph of the rabble ("el triunfo de la gentualla"). See *Argentina 1930-1960*, pp. 27, 31.

[9] Olguín, *Dos políticos y dos políticas*, pp. 117-135; *Lencinas*, p. 304.

forthcoming election of 1921. Desiring the governorship himself, C. W. Lencinas, oldest son of José Nestor Lencinas and then provincial president of the Mendocino Radical Civic Union, formed his own independent political party—the Lencinist Radical Civic Union. C. W. Lencinas won the election and assumed the governorship in 1922.

In 1922 Marcelo T. de Alvear, the new Radical president of Argentina, intervened Mendoza only because the intervention decree had already been signed by Yrigoyen before ending his term. Believing Alvear to be a manageable subordinate, Yrigoyen had selected Alvear as the next president. However, in 1924 Alvear and other Radical leaders, opposed to Yrigoyen's continued direction of the party, withdrew from the Radical Civic Union and formed their own Anti-personalist Radical Party.[10] But no separate party was formed in Mendoza Province because the cordial relations between Alvear and C. W. Lencinas meant that the Lencinist movement performed this function locally. The policy of Alvear was not to interfere in the provincial parties' affairs. Alvear named an interventor in Mendoza in 1924 because of administrative corruption by the provincial government and not because of internal party conflicts. Thus, in the gubernatorial election of 1926 the Lencinas Party easily elected its candidate. Re-elected president in 1928, Yrigoyen intervened Mendoza in order to crush the Lencinist faction and to assure control of the Mendocino Radical party by the national leadership in Buenos Aires. On November 10, 1929, Carlos Washington Lencinas was assassinated by a Radical follower of Yrigoyen.[11]

The significance of the assassination of C. W. Lencinas is twofold. First, it created a public indignation in Argentina conducive to the Revolution of 1930.[12] Second, it signified the type of methods necessary to achieve subordination of a provincial party leadership by the national party leadership within a political party. The characteristic of all these interventions by Yrigoyen, in his attempt to control or to sub-ordinate an independently acting provincial party, is their failure. In each conflict the national leadership lost, and the provincial leadership maintained its autonomy. These unsuccessful interventions simply serve as

[10] The Anti-personalist Radical Party was formed on August 23, 1924, and two years later had created its own national organization. The party never developed into an effectively separate political organization; its effectiveness was more in the nature of "palace intrigue" than as an electoral opposition. The common motive was internal opposition to Yrigoyen's domination of the party. Other reasons were disputes over candidacies, party electoral policy, and the socio-economic policies of Yrigoyen. See del Mazo, *El radicalismo*, II, pp. 29-36; *Félix Luna*, Yrigoyen, pp. 309-314; Rennie, *The Argentine Republic*, p. 221; Snow, *Argentine Radicalism*, p. 42.

[11] Scalvini, *Historia de Mendoza*, pp. 386-390; Luna, *Yrigoyen*, pp. 303-326; Olguín, *Lencinas*, pp. 384-389, 497; José H. Lencinas, *Economía y política*, pp. 108, 119-125, 132.

[12] Luna, *Yrigoyen*, p. 276.

an indication that the national leader did not manage the whole party authoritatively, but at times had to adapt himself to provincial party leaders and to party situations over which he had no control.

The third period in the political history of Mendoza started with the Revolution of September 6, 1930. The bases and the explanations of the contemporary political developments of Mendoza, as of Argentina, were created by this Revolution. The Radical explanation for the cause of the Revolution was that to hold provincial elections on September 7, 1930, in the Provinces of San Juan and Mendoza would have meant the selection of four Radical national senators from these provinces and would have given the Radical Civic Union a majority in the Senate for the first time during the government of Yrigoyen and Alvear. Yrigoyen would, thus, have been able to nationalize Argentina's petroleum.[13] There were probably several causes for the 1930 Revolution. One was the economic conditions caused by the Great Depression. Another was the senility of Yrigoyen, who had become President in 1928 when seventy-six years old. A third reason was the extensive corruption practiced by the Radical government. A fourth was the long-time opposition of elements of the military to any government headed by Yrigoyen. All of these factors meant that generally the country had lost confidence in the Radical government, as shown in the March, 1930, elections in the Federal Capital, elections which the Radicals lost for the first time in fifteen years.[14]

The 1930 Revolution was to result in government by the conservative political and economic elements in Argentina under the leadership of the National Democratic Party until 1943. These thirteen years of Conservative government, both national and provincial, were made possible by two conditions. One condition was the systematic use of electoral fraud to create an electoral majority for a popular minority. The other condition was the creation of an effective coalition of political parties which co-operated in the national and provincial legislatures as well as in the national and provincial elections. This coalition was known as the Concordancia and consisted of the National Democratic Party, the Independent Socialist Party, and Anti-personalist Radical Party, and some independent provincial parties. The Concordancia elected Agustín P. Justo in the presidential election of 1931 and Roberto Ortiz in the election of 1937.[15]

[13] Del Mazo, *El radicalismo*, II, p. 141.

[14] Luis Campoy, "Factors That Led to the Successful Revolt of 1930 and the Revolution of 1943 in Argentina," p. 18; Snow, *Argentine Radicalism*, pp. 44-45.

[15] *Argentina 1930-1960*, pp. 40, 110-111. This period of political history is known as the Decade of Concord ("Década Concordancista") by its supporters or as the Infamous Decade ("Década Infame") by its worst critics. The Democrats justified the use of fraud as necessary and regarded themselves as patriots who saved the nation ("salvadores de la patria").

Formed in 1917, the Mendocino Conservative Party adopted the name of Liberal Party during the 1920's; and although very active, the party was indecisive in the provincial politics because of its small electoral vote. In 1931 the Conservative Party of Buenos Aires Province initiated conversations with other provincial conservative groups to form a national party. In August of 1931 the National Democratic Party was formed as a federation of independent provincial parties to support a common presidential candidate and policy program at the national level, but in which each provincial party was independent within its province in the selection of candidates and in the formulation and achievement of its party platform. The Mendocino Liberal Party joined this federation, accepting the name of National Democratic Party.

All Mendocino political parties experienced a series of internal conflicts and factionalism, caused by the adjustment to the new political and electoral reality imposed by the 1930 Revolution. From 1933 until 1938 the Mendocino National Democratic Party was divided into the blue faction and the white faction. This factional conflict stemmed essentially from the problem of how many legislative candidates and administrative appointments were to be decided by each faction, now that the Conservatives were the provincial governing party. The conflict started with the internal party election of July of 1933 in which the blue faction elected a majority of the provincial party leadership. Personally piqued by the loss of the internal election and unhappy because they would now control fewer administrative appointments and fewer legislative and executive positions, the white leaders aggressively sought to increase their share of the legislative candidacies or belligerently refused to co-operate in the conduct of the party or the provincial government. In 1937 the white leaders resurrected the former Liberal Party, but it soon disappeared with the resignation of its own leaders. In January of 1938 the provincial leaders of the white and the blue factions achieved a satisfactory compromise to share the gubernatorial and legislative candidates. Probably the most significant factor in ending this internal party conflict was the need to maintain party unity. Although the Concordancia elected its candidate Roberto Ortiz in the presidential election of 1937, the Radical Civic Union gained a majority of the national deputies.[16]

[16] Roberto Ortiz belonged to the Anti-personalist Radical Party and was a well-known corporation lawyer who had been Minister of Public Works during the presidency of Alvear (1922-1928) and Minister of Finance during the presidency of Justo (1931-1937). The Radical Civic Union Party was passive in the presidential election of 1937 because of a secret understanding between President Justo and the national Radical leaders that Ortiz would be elected President. Simultaneously, the national Radical leaders made a secret understanding with Ortiz that if he were elected, he would help the Radical Civic Union Party back into power. See Rennie, *The Argentine Republic*, p. 262.

The internal party dispute within the Mendocino National Democratic Party is instructive in three senses. First, the provincial leadership of the blue faction—which represented the party majority—was forced to concede continually to the minority, rather than being able unconditionally and automatically to impose its wishes upon the minority. For example, the majority resigned its positions of the provincial party leadership in 1934 to allow the white leaders to assume control of the party, or it accepted the white faction's choice of the gubernatorial candidate in 1935. Second, national leaders of the party attempted to end the provincial party dispute during the years 1933-1935 by means of acting as arbitrators or "friends of the court." The characteristics of all these efforts by national leaders is that they succeeded only to the extent and willingness with which they were accepted by provincial party leaders. National party leaders were unable to impose their own decisions upon the provincial party. Third, memory of this profoundly disruptive factional dispute remains today and partly explains why Democratic Party leaders are unwilling to experience internal party elections with their consequent disruptive factional effects.

While the National Democratic Party adjusted to the reality that now it was the governing party, the Radical Civic Union adjusted to the reality that now it was the opposition party. First, the Mendocino Radical Party, like the national Radical Party, reorganized and re-structured the provincial party under the direction of a provincial Committee of Re-organization. The party was reorganized, for the first time, upon the basis of published lists of members who elected directly the party authorities of each department and the provincial party officials in an internal party election.[17]

Secondly, the Mendocino Radical Party, like the national Radical Party, initially adopted a policy of electoral abstention. Under this policy the provincial and national party organizations refrained from presenting any candidates in any election and required their membership to abstain from voting in any election, although in the 1931 election the membership was allowed to cast blank ballots. The Radical party abstained electorally from the 1931 election until the 1936 election, and the Mendocino party initially was one of the strong supporters of the policy of electoral abstention. This policy of electoral abstention was not new to the Radical party, as it had been used for fifteen years from 1898 until 1912 when certain provincial parties decided to participate electorally with or without the required consent of the national party leaders. All Radical leaders were agreed by 1935 that electoral abstention was an absurd and suicidal policy which was causing the party to

[17] These concepts and their practices were first used in the Radical Civic Union in the 1930's and were later extended to the Democratic Party and to the Neo-Peronists parties after the Revolution of 1955.

lose its membership and its significance. Unfortunately, however, electoral participation caused the Radical party to become increasingly concerned solely with gaining elections and crushing internal criticism and disagreement by arguing of the need to unite party forces for electoral victory. Its electoral participation, in effect, meant that the Radical Civic Union legalized the 1930 Revolution and its subsequent governments.[18]

Thirdly, the Mendocino Radical party, like the national party, was characterized by a series of internal factional disputes to determine control of the provincial party. From 1932 until 1948 the Alvear faction managed the Radical Party nationally with the purpose of eliminating the Yrigoyen faction from national direction of the party, chiefly by two methods: first, the use of electoral fraud and intervention to remove Yrigoyenists from control of the party organs, and sometimes their subsequent exclusion from the party in order to eliminate any criticism; and second, the incorporation of formerly independent Radical movements into the party as a means of reducing the Yrigoyenist majority.[19] These disputes did not begin until 1936 when the Mendocino Radical party participated electorally for the first time. These disputes did not achieve the high degree of virulence or an open breach between Alvearists and Yrigoyenists as in other provincial parties. The main reason was the essentially conservative orientation of Mendocino Radicalism, which meant the absence of serious ideological controversy. The other reason was that the disputes were not between followers of Alvear versus the followers of Yrigoyen, but were between former Yrigoyenist leaders for the party's presidency. In 1936 Rubén Palero Infante and Tomás González Funes won control of the provincial party in an internal election against a faction which had combined with the newly admitted bulk of the Lencinist members. This election meant that during the 1930's, Mendocino Radicalism was directed by Tomás González Funes, who managed party affairs in the Southern half of the province, and by Rubén Palero Infante, who managed party affairs in the Northern half of the province. Opposing leaders were ignored by the provincial leadership, except at election time, or were suspended from membership when their criticism of party orientation or party direction became too insistent. Palero Infante was supported in his management of the Mendocino party by Alvear and the national party leadership, who ignored appeals by opposing provincial leaders to end questionable electoral procedures by the Provincial Committee.

By the beginning of the 1940's the Mendocino Radicalism—like the

[18] Luna, *Alvear*, pp. 142-143, 156. This same attitude was also shared by many leaders and members of the Mendocino Radical Party. See *Los Andes*, 19 April 1941, p. 7.

[19] Luna, *Alvear*, pp. 144-145; del Mazo, *El radicalismo*, II, p. 170; Rodolfo Puiggrós, *Historia crítica de los partidos políticos*, p. 404.

national Radicalism—experienced a feeling of frustration and the need to develop new ideas and policies. This desire to renovate party management and party orientation was reflected by the younger generation of party leaders when they won two internal party elections against Palero Infante in 1941. Palero Infante then invited these young leaders to share the party leadership with him. These elections in 1941 initiated the careers of the present leadership of the Mendocino Radical parties.

Alvear quit the presidency of the national Radical Civic Union, disillusioned by political party activity and with the realization that his leadership had been one of escape and sterility after the 1930 Revolution. The great error of Alvear was not that he failed to lead an armed counter-revolution against the government or that he ended the Yrigoyenist policy of electoral abstention. His error was that he failed to renovate the Radical party ideologically by developing a new social and economic program which would awaken popular enthusiasm and which would attract the rising working class and the new intellectuals. In effect, Alvear and the Alvearist faction missed their historic moment and contented themselves with demands for electoral honesty and constitutional correctness rather than demands for change and fundamental social reform.[20] However, the Radical involution under Alvear produced its own reactions within the party. The first was the formation of F.O.R.J.A. in 1935, a movement of Yrigoyenist leaders who developed new party policy and orientation by a series of research studies and debates. F.O.R.J.A. never gained support within the Mendocino party; it was more a movement of the Litoral Provinces, which split in 1945 between those who were to incorporate themselves into Peronism and those who formed the Movement of Intransigence and Renovation under Arturo Frondizi and sought to obtain control of the party internally.[21] The second was the election of Amadeo Sabattini as Radical governor of Córdoba in 1936, where he initiated an impressive program of public improvements and social welfare. The governorship of Sabattini caused the formation within Radicalism of a movement which wished to emulate Sabattini's experience in other provinces. This movement, known as National Intransigence, never developed decisive support within the Mendocino Radicalism. After 1934 the incomprehension of the socio-economic problems of Argentina meant that Radicalism was to become one of the opposing forces to Peronism in the Election of 1946.[22]

The third major political movement of Mendoza Province, the Lencinists, never adjusted to the new political reality imposed by the

[20] Luna, *Alvear,* pp. 182-187; Rennie, *The Argentine Republic,* pp. 341-342; Moisés Lebensohn, *Pensamiento y acción,* p. 151.

[21] Alberto Ciria, *Partidos y poder en la Argentina moderna (1930-1946),* pp. 148, 154, 171-172.

[22] *Ibid.,* p. 149.

1930 Revolution. One reason was systematic persecution of Lencinists by the National Democratic Party, which denied the movement electoral recognition until 1934. The major reason, however, was the failure of the Lencinist Party to develop strong constructive leadership after the assassination of Carlos Washington Lencinas. The younger brothers, José Hipólito Lencinas and Rafael Néstor Lencinas, assumed direction of the movement as their own personal fief, because of their family name. But they lacked the political ability, the flexibility, and the altruism of their father and older brother. Their dispute with each other for management of the party soon degenerated into personal rivalry and caused a profound split within the party. Equating efforts to re-unify with the national Radical Party as personal disloyalty to himself, José H. Lencinas expelled a majority of the provincial leaders from his own party. They thereupon joined the national Radical party in 1935. In 1937, displeased with internal party practices and ideological orientation of the Mendocino Radical Party, another faction of former Lencinist members formed their own independent party.[23] In 1946 the bulk of the Lencinist leaders and members incorporated themselves massively into the Peronist movement. After the Revolution of 1955 efforts by José Hipólito Lencinas to revive the movement as an independent political party failed for lack of enough members to gain electoral recognition. Lencinas and the Lencinist Movement had become a historical memory.

The last major party affected by the Revolution of 1930 and its subsequent events was the Socialist Party. Argentine Socialism began in 1881 when a group of German Socialist immigrants started a workers' association in Buenos Aires, known as the club "Vorwarts." In 1895 in Buenos Aires this and other clubs of immigrant Socialists founded the Argentine Socialist Workers Party, which became the present-day Socialist party. Although essentially a party of the Federal Capital and the Province of Buenos Aires, the Socialist Party did develop important movements in the Interior Provinces of Córdoba, Santa Fe, San Juan, and Mendoza.[24] Initiated in 1912 in the provincial Capital under the leadership of Ramón Morey, the Socialist Party elected Morey its first provincial deputy in the 1914 Election and also the largest minority of provincial delegates who wrote the Provincial Constitution of 1916. During the 1920's the Socialists formed the majority opposition party to Radicalism. The 1930 Revolution caused an ideological conflict within the Mendocino party between a majority of members led by Benito Marianetti, who favored an armed counter-revolution against the Na-

[23] *Los Andes,* 18 May 1937, p. 4; 15 July 1937, p. 4.
[24] Benito Marianetti, *Argentina: realidad . . .,* p. 378. Marianetti was the first member from an Interior Province [Mendoza] elected to the National Executive Committee of the Socialist Party in 1934. Previously, the National Committee had consisted of only delegates from the Federal Capital or the Province of Buenos Aires.

tional Democratic government, and a minority who favored the traditional democratic evolutionary tactics of Argentine Socialism. Meeting in 1934 at Santa Fe, the National Congress, consisting of provincial representatives, supported the national party leadership and its doctrine of democratic evolution. In 1937 the national leadership expelled the Mendocino party. The provincial party, under the leadership of Benito Marianetti, joined with other likeminded provincial Socialist groups to form the Socialist Workers Party. This party existed until 1943, controlling the Department of Godoy Cruz, where it initiated a series of noteworthy public improvements and social welfare measures. In 1945 the Party incorporated itself into the Communist Party.[25] During the government of Perón, Socialist and Communist parties, provincially as well as nationally, were systematically persecuted. However, the Socialists presented candidates until the 1951 elections, despite only a minimum of votes. In 1958 the Socialist Party split into the Democratic Socialist Party, which opposed electoral participation by the Peronists' movements, and the Argentine Socialist Party, which opposed electoral exclusion of the Peronists. Practically all of the Mendocino Socialists joined the Argentine Socialist Party. In Mendoza the Socialists remained an significant electoral force after 1958 only as long as the Peronists were effectively excluded from electoral participation or were unable to unite effectively. Their electoral strength was the Third District, from which the Socialists elected one provincial deputy in the 1963 Election.[26]

The Revolution of June 4, 1943, initiated the fourth and present period in the political history of Mendoza—as well as of Argentina. The Revolution of 1943 marked the end of the society initiated by the Battle of Pavón, its economy, and its way of life. The Revolution marked the end of Argentina of an enlightened Oligarchy, its liberal free trader, and the aspiration, power and predominance of the landed aristocracy. The causes of the Revolution were several. The blindness of President Ortiz by July of 1940 forced him to abandon the national government to his Vice-president Ramón Castillo. Castillo relied upon the traditional state of seige, provincial intervention, and publically

[25] *Los Andes,* 11 January 1937, p. 1; 12 January 1937, p. 4; 1 March 1937, p. 12. The author does not know when the Communist Party was founded in Mendoza. The first newspaper reference to the party was in *Los Andes,* 25 January 1930, p. 8.

[26] One criticism of the Argentine Socialist Party has been the internal contradiction between its principles and its practices. The party's principles and ideology are revolutionary and seek to change the existing capitalistic system of Argentina. But the party's methods are evolutionary and legalistic and aim to operate within the existing legal system. This contradiction may have caused the party to lose force and purpose. See Silvio Frondizi, *Doce años de política Argentina,* p. 59.

admitted electoral fraud as the means to maintain his increasingly un-popular government. Castillo's choice of Robustiano Patrón Costas, wealthy sugar grower of Salta, as his presidential successor for the forthcoming Election of 1943 aroused widespread public antagonism.[27]

These culminating events of a period of electoral fraud and authoritarian government caused a feeling of desperation and futility expressed by means of a widespread public lethargy. After 1939 this feeling was reflected in Mendoza Province in that an increasing number of persons did not vote in the provincial elections. In the 1942 election the non-voting population exceeded more than 55% in some Departments. This casual attitude became so widespread that the Mendocino National Democratic Party published an open letter reminding the citizenry that it was their civic duty to vote and abhoring the citizens' indifference to politics. What the letter failed to say was that, in effect, it was the civic duty of the citizenry to participate in an undemocratic, fraudulent electoral system. Perhaps this letter represented a certain cynicism, or perhaps it represented the true sentiments of a political group which had become too accustomed to fraud. Simultaneously, there appeared in the provincial newspapers statements by political leaders and political parties about the need to end electoral fraud and to return to the condition of political civil rights. All such statements generally concluded with the idea that Argentina was at the start of another historical moment when a great leader would appear who would represent the popular will and who would implement civic legality.

In January of 1943 a group of citizens met and initiated a new political party, the Republican National Party, whose platform was a combination of nationalism and socio-economic reform. The party advocated the formation of leaders who would represent the popular will of the masses and would return the society to its historically great national traditions. The party advocated widespread improvement in the conditions of the workers and economic-industrial development to create new sources of employment. These incidents indicated a preceding atmosphere and state of mind which made the coming of Perón seem a most natural event.[28]

Simultaneously, the Second World War was to divide Argentines intellectually and emotionally between those who favored England and the Allied Cause and those who favored Germany and the Axis Cause. The sector which regarded England as fighting to defend Western civilization from a totalitarian aggressor formed Argentine Action. Another sector, which favored Germany as a reaction against Argentina's condition as an economic colony of England and which wanted

[27] Rennie, *The Argentine Republic*, p. 344. Snow, *Argentine Radicalism*, p. 58.
[28] *Los Andes*, 20 October 1941, p. 9; 8 February 1942, p. 7; 2 March 1942, p. 7; 23 January 1943, p. 5.

to develop Argentina economically and industrially, formed the National Alliance of Restoration. An absence of the spirit and mental attitude of neutrality which had prevailed during the First World War meant that any government's action would automatically be repudiated by a significant sector of the population.[29] The national and provincial governments had lost effective contact with the popular reality. Furthermore, a new industrial class and a new industrial mass had developed in Argentina. The great Depression had depreciated the peso and forced Argentina to manufacture many things it could no longer afford to purchase abroad; likewise, after 1939, the country was isolated from its former markets and had to rely upon its own production. This industrialization meant that one million persons (one-fifth of Argentina's rural population) emigrated to urban areas, essentially Buenos Aires. Manufactures were replacing agriculture as the country's source of wealth. The military leaders, who revolted in 1943 under the leadership of General Pedro Ramírez, were middle class in origin and belief and opposed not only the landed Oligarchy of the 1930's but feared the working class and a possible proletarian revolution.[30]

Named Secretary of Labor in 1943, Juan Perón made a concentrated effort from the beginning to gain support of the laboring classes of the country. Many were converted to Perón because they believed that his government was one of the few ever interested in the condition of the workers.[31] From 1943 until the Presidential Elections of 1946 Perón sought to gain the collaboration of various political parties.[32] In 1945 the national Radical leader, Juan H. Quijano, accepted a cabinet position as Minister of Interior in the Perón-Farrell Government. Expelled from the Radical Civic Union, Quijano formed the

[29] Luna, *Alvear*, pp. 263-267. In Mendoza Province the leaders of Argentine Action were the major provincial leaders of the Socialist, National Democratic, and the Radical Civic Union Parties. See *Los Andes*, 19 August 1940, p. 5; 17 May 1941, p. 5.

[30] Rennie, *The Argentine Republic*, pp. 327, 356-357; Campobassi and others, *Los partidos políticos: estructura y vigencia en la Argentina*, pp. 43-44.

[31] George Blanksten, *Perón's Argentina*, p. 258; Walter B. Allende, *El fracaso de Perón y el problema argentino*, pp. 18-22.

[32] Several times Perón attempted to attract the support of other political parties. In October of 1943 Perón's offer of all cabinet positions (except the military) was rejected by the national leaders of the Radical Civic Union. Then Perón attempted to enlist the support of the Communists. In 1945 Perón made the following offer to the national leaders of the Radical Civic Union in preparation for the presidential election of 1946: 1) the Radicals were to receive all provincial gubernatorial positions; 2) the Radicals were to receive the majority of national legislators; 3) and the Radicals were to receive the Vice-presidency. In return, the Radicals would support the presidential candidacy of Perón. Perón, and others, feared that the Radicals were the most popular party at this time and would be unbeatable in an election. See Juan J. Real, *30 años de historia argentina*, pp. 68, 85.

Radical Civic Union Council of Renovation, its purpose to allow Radicals to enter the Revolutionary Government and to support the presidential candidacy of Perón.

In August, 1945, Mendocino Radicals who were in agreement with the 1943 Revolution and the policies of Perón, formed a separate Commission of Reorganization, began to organize throughout Mendoza Province, and in November, 1945, formally joined the national movement of Quijano. On October 24, 1945, Perón founded his own Labor Party, which was formed one month later in Mendoza by provincial labor union leaders. This party was to allow union leaders and members, former Democratics and Socialists, and independent persons to support the presidential candidacy of Perón.[33]

Perón was elected president by a national majority in the election of February of 1946, as well as in Mendoza Province, against the Democratic Union, an electoral front of the Radical, Socialist, Communist, and Democratic Progressive Parties to support the Radical presidential candidates. Efforts by the Socialist and Communist Parties to nominate common candidates in the provincial elections in Mendoza Province failed because of the refusal of the Radicals. Electoral fronts had become common among political parties after 1930. In the Election of 1931 the Socialists and the Democratic Progressives formed the Democratic-Socialist Alliance to support common presidential candidates as well as common gubernatorial and legislative candidates in Mendoza Province. In the Election of 1941 the two parties, the Radical Civic Union and the Radical Civic Union of Mendoza, nominated common gubernatorial candidates in Mendoza Province, although the Radical Civic Union had previously refused to participate in electoral fronts except to the extent of presenting common candidates in departmental elections or of abstaining in departmental elections in favor of the dominant party. In preparation for the presidential Election of 1943 the Radicals, Socialists, and Democratic Progressives formed a national Democratic Union to oppose the candidacy of Robustiano Patrón Costas. These electoral pacts were always opposed by the Yrigoyenist faction of the Radical Party, while the Alvearist faction generally favored electoral pacts. Those who favored these electoral pacts became known as "Unionists" within the Radical Civic Union.[34]

Originally Perón had been elected by two independent political parties: his own Labor Party and the Radical Civic Union Council of Renovation. From the beginning these two parties were in conflict, although the two parties had nominated common gubernatorial and

[33] *Los Andes,* 25 August 1945, p. 7; 1 November 1945, p. 5; 18 November 1945, p. 4; and private interviews by the author.

[34] Del Mazo, III, p. 290. The Mendocino Radical Party has always been a stronghold of this "Unionist" sentiment, and the present Mendocino Party is dominated by these "Unionists."

legislative candidates in 1946. Initially, disagreement developed as to the number of legislative candidates to be selected by each party. The Labor leaders understood that they were to choose one-half of the candidates, while the Peronist Radicals felt that they should choose a majority of the candidates.[35] After the election of Perón the disputes between the two Mendocino parties became more violent. First, the Labor leaders felt that they were defrauded when the Peronist Radicals selected two of their own members to both national senatorships from Mendoza Province.[36] Second, the Labor leaders felt that the Peronist Radicals systematically occupied a majority of directive positions within the new Party of the National Revolution formed by Perón to unify the two former parties. The third, and by far the major, dispute was the contention of the Labor leaders that officials and members of their party were systematically excluded from occupying administrative posts by the Peronist Radicals. Feeling that the Peronist Radicals were intentionally using the Peronist movement for their own benefit, the Labor leaders and legislators refused to participate wholeheartedly in the Party and maintained their own party organization and presented their own legislative candidates in the provincial Elections of 1947 and 1948. The disputes ended after the forceful fusion of the two parties into the Peronist Party in 1949 under the rigidly vertical leadership of Perón, and Perón's appointment of Blas Brisoli as governor of Mendoza Province in 1949 in order to break the dominance of the Radical Peronists.

The Perón Government lasted from 1946 until its overthrow by the Revolution of September 16, 1955. After 1952 the Peronist Party became increasingly dominated by Alberto Teisaire, a Mendocino who was national Vice-president, as well as president of the Peronist National Superior Council. During the Perón Government only the Radical Civic Union continued to function as an organized and articulate opposition party within Mendoza Province, while the National Democratic Party and the Socialist movements withdrew from electoral activity after the Election of November, 1951.

During the years 1944 and 1945 there developed various provincial groups within the Radical Civic Union, which wished to renovate the leadership as well as the ideological principles of the party. These groups met and formed the Movement of Intransigence and Renovation in April of 1945, and by 1948 this internal faction had gained control of the national party organization and most provincial parties. In an unsuccessful effort to stop the Intransigents, the Unionists formed their

[35] Eventually an agreement was made whereby candidacies for six deputies and three senators were reserved for the Peronist Radicals to fill with "qualified men with special necessary abilities" for the legislative role. The remainder of the legislative candidacies were divided half and half between the two parties.

[36] Originally, the agreement was that the Peronist Radicals would select a candidate and the Labor leaders would select a candidate.

own national party organization known as the "Unity" faction, whose base of strength was Mendoza Province where the Intransigents never developed a decisive following except in the Department of San Rafael under the leadership of Ernesto Ueltschi.[37] The dispute between the Intransigents and the other party factions concerned the Radical's presidential nominee: the Intransigents wanted Arturo Frondizi to be the presidential candidate in the elections following the 1955 Revolution; the Unionists and other factions were opposed to the candidacy of Frondizi. In November of 1956 the party's National Convention nominated Frondizi and Alejandro Gómez as its presidential candidates. The Unionist delegates from Mendoza refused to participate in this National Convention; in the provincial Congress on December 3, 1956, the Mendocino Radicals repudiated the presidential formula and declared the Mendocino party independent of the national party. The national leaders intervened in the Mendocino party—the first provincial party to be intervened—and when this intervention was ignored by the provincial leaders, the national leaders expelled the provincial leadership from the party. On February 14, 1957, these expelled Mendocino leaders formed their own national party, to be known as the Popular Radical Civic Union, consisting of provincial groups of Unionists, Sabbattinists, and Balbinists (followers of Ricardo Balbín). A provincial party Congress approved this action of the Mendocino leadership. In effect, the Radical supporters of Frondizi in Mendoza Province found themselves excluded and necessarily had to create their own effective political party organization, which was to be known as the Intransigent Radical Civic Union.[38]

In the election of February 23, 1958, the U.C.R.I. gained the presidency for Frondizi and elected Ernesto Ueltschi governor of Mendoza Province, with the national—as well as the provincial—support of the Peronist voters.[39] Internal party frictions essentially explain why the

[37] Del Mazo, *El radicalismo,* III, pp. 45, 50, 64; *Los Andes,* 12 November 1945, p. 13; 14 December 1949, p. 7; 10 December 1950, p. 4; 19 April 1955, p. 4; Moisés Lebensohn, *Pensamiento y acción,* pp. xxix-xxx.

[38] Del Mazo, *El radicalismo,* III, pp. 276-285; *Los Andes,* 26 November 1956, p. 5; 3 December 1956, p. 3; 4 December 1956, p. 1; 31 January 1957, p. 6; 14 February 1957, p. 1; 16 February 1957, p. 1; 7 March 1957, p. 4. The "Unionist" argument was that Frondizi did not represent the popular will of the Radical membership and that Frondizi should submit to a direct primary election within the party. This same argument was used by the minority factions within the Radical Civic Union in opposition to the pre-candidacy of Alvear in 1937. See Snow, *Argentine Radicalism,* p. 73.

[39] *Los Andes,* 20 February 1958, p. 5. The Peronists voted for the U.C.R.I. candidates upon the basis of an electoral agreement signed by Perón and John William Cooke with Frondizi and Rogelio Frigerio. The instructions for the Peronists to vote for the U.C.R.I. were carried by a former provincial deputy and future national deputy, who was captured by the Argentine Army Intelligence when he entered Mendoza Province from Chile. Frondizi has always denied that

Mendocino U.C.R.I. lost in the elections of 1959 to the Democrats whereas other provincial governments of the U.C.R.I. gained electorally. One cause of friction was ideological: the Radical youth under Ueltschi were concerned to develop new programs, while the older, senior Radicals were concerned with the re-unification of all Radicals and with administrative efficiency and honesty. Administrative appointments in the provincial government were a major cause of friction. Initially, Ueltschi favored members of his faction or former Peronists in his governmental designations, but after the losses in the Elections of 1959 and 1960 he was forced to appoint members of the opposing faction as a means of gaining their support. The third cause of friction was over candidacies: Ueltschi and his followers, as well as the national senators of U.C.R.I., favored one candidate in the provincial gubernatorial election of 1961; while the older, senior Radicals favored another candidacy.[40] In the election of 1961 the Democrats elected the governor. This electoral loss, coupled with the overthrow of Frondizi by the Revolt of 1962, caused the Intransigent party to divide and by 1966 the bulk of the older senior Radicals had re-affiliated with the U.C.R.P. Party. The remaining Intransigents either tacitly or publicly supported the Peronists.[41]

Formed in 1958 initially by an opposition to the presidential candidacy of Frondizi, the U.C.R.P. never formed an effective opposition party in Mendoza Province until the Democratic victory of 1961. Afterward, the U.C.R.P. increasingly occupied the position of the third party after the Democrats and Peronists—even with the return of former Intransigents. This condition caused an internal dispute between the "Recuperation" Faction, which criticized the leadership of the provincial party by the "Popular Cause" Faction. The name "Recuperation" refers to the desire to recover the traditional party principles and the former electoral vigor of Radicalism, as developed by Alem and Yrigoyen. The faction's strength was in the Second Electoral District, until it failed to gain even minority representation in that District in the internal party election of 1965.

The other party included in this investigation is the Christian

---

he signed the electoral pact initiated by Rogelio Frigerio before the 1958 election. See Luna, *Diálogos con Frondizi*, p. 40.

[40] The two factions which formed the Mendocino U.C.R.I. never really fused, but essentially remained as temporarily united independent factions. An attempt was made to manage the party by means of a co-ordinating Council of Political Party Action (J.A.P.P.) in which both factions were equally represented by their major provincial leaders. However, the Mendocino U.C.R.I. remained essentially an anarchic party in which Governor Ueltschi was often opposed by the provincial legislators of U.C.R.I.

[41] Leaders of U.C.R.P., whom the author interviewed, stated that between 10,000 and 15,000 members of U.C.R.I. were re-affiliated.

Democrat Party. This party began secretly in Mendoza Province in 1954 under the leadership of Ricardo Dussell, who had participated in the founding meeting of the national party in July of 1954 in Rosario. Initially, the Mendocino party did not participate electorally for lack of candidates and financial resources. Many of the original leaders of the Mendocino party have become inactive because of their opposition to the party's former national president's policy of co-operation with the Peronists.

The Democrats emerged from the 1955 Revolution to find that many members had joined with the Peronists or Radicals, that the party had been thoroughly repudiated electorally, and that the party was split between the National Democrats, still managed by the party leaders of the 1930's, and the Popular Conservative Democrats of the younger membership and leaders. Several factors, however, caused the Democrats to recover as a major party in Mendoza Province. One was the failure of the U.C.R.I. Government, causing many voters to turn to the Democrats as the least undesirable alternative. (In 1959 the Democrats elected a group of provincial legislators who discharged a noteworthy role.) A second factor was an internal movement within the party to give the party new leadership and a new orientation. This group of newer and younger elements, although it lost the 1960 internal party election to choose the gubernatorial candidate to the older senior leaders, did succeed in forcing the older leadership to give the party a new image by co-opting newer and younger elements into leadership positions and by adopting a new ideology of social welfare.[42] The third factor was that, once in power, the Democrats discharged an efficient and progressive administration, in contrast to the experience of the 1930's.[43] In 1958 the Democrats joined the Federation of Parties of the Center, a loose national confederation of provincial Conservative parties. By 1960 the bulk of membership of the Mendocino Popular Conservative Democrats has rejoined the Democrat Party.

After the Revolution of 1955 the Peronists were prohibited from political participation and the Peronist Party was dissolved, although

[42] This change is evidenced by the situation within the Democratic Party in which persons having the same family names as party leaders of the 1930's feel that they face a greater handicap to be selected as candidates, especially if they are from Mendocino creole families. Also, many Democrats interviewed by the author stated that in 1960 a faction's original pre-candidate had to withdraw from the candidacy because he had developed a certain unpopular reputation due to his activity within the Democratic Party during the 1930's.

[43] See Luna, *Diálogos con Frondizi*, p. 124. Many Democrats interviewed by the author stated that the party had learned its lesson under the Perón Government, which had been caused as a reaction to the reactionary policies and electoral fraud practiced by the Democrats during the 1930's. The feeling of these Democrats was that it was the party's responsibility to govern so well that there could be no desire to return to Peronism.

the Peronists maintained their organization informally. In the initial elections the Mendocino Peronists, like the national movement, voted blank ballots as their form of protest or voted for Frondizi in the Election of 1958. In December of 1960 certain political leaders withdrew from the Peronist movement and formed their own independent political party in Mendoza Province, known as Tres Banderas. This type of autonomous provincial party started in Mendoza Province and initiated what was known as the "Hard Line of Mendoza": that is, an independent provincial party which refused to accept control or direction from either Perón or from the national leadership of the Peronist movement in Buenos Aires. The reason for this development was the attitude of Mendocino leaders that the policy of protesting by means of blank votes was causing the Peronist Movement to degenerate, as a frustrated membership increasingly turned to other political parties as a means of expressing their desires. Furthermore, these leaders felt that the Peronist Movement could become an effective political force best by democratic electoral participation rather than by armed revolt or terrorism.[44] Tres Banderas participated in the election of 1961, while the loyal followers of Perón voted blank ballots. In response to the formation of Tres Banderas, the national leaders of the Peronist Movement recognized the Blanco Party as the official Peronist Party in Mendoza Province and allowed it to present candidates.[45]

In 1962 the Frondizi Government was overthrown by an army revolt. The decision of Frondizi to allow the Peronists to participate freely in the Election of 1962, without any proscriptions, resulted in the electoral victory of the Peronists, especially in the Province of Buenos Aires. Their victory caused a certain sector of the army to revolt. Afterwards, the provisional government convoked national and provincial elections on July 7, 1963, under a series of new electoral regulations. In this election the Democrat Party won the governorship with the support of the U.C.R.P. Party, the Peronists gained control of the

[44] This attitude was expressed by the Declaration of Avellaneda of October, 1965, one of whose initiators was a major Peronist leader of Mendoza. See *Le Nación,* 20 October 1965, p. 6. The gubernatorial election of 1966 in which the Mendocino Peronists split into two factions, each supporting its own candidate, was partly a referendum within Peronism over this declaration. One candidacy represented that faction which sought to institutionalize the Peronist movement. One candidacy represented that faction which was concerned to retain the traditional vertical leadership under Perón.

[45] The Blanco Party had been founded in 1958 as a provincial party but did not become an active party presenting its own candidates until 1962. The other Peronist Party in Mendoza Province was the Popular Union Party, the only nationally organized Peronist Party which functioned within Mendoza Province. However, its role has been minimal except as a refuge for the disheartened and discarded leaders of the other provincial Peronist parties. The significant Peronist leaders preferred to function within the Blanco Party.

provincial legislature with the support of the U.C.R.P. Party, and the Radicals chose the two national senators from Mendoza Province with the support of the two other parties. After the election of 1963, the provincial leaders of the Blanco and Tres Banderas signed an agreement forming a unified political party, the Popular Movement of Mendoza.[46] Fear of a Peronist victory in Mendoza Province in the forthcoming election of 1965 meant that the Justicialist (Justice) Party was granted electoral recognition in Mendoza Province. In the legislative elections of 1965 the Peronists, together, won an overwhelming vote. Then the Democrats and the U.C.R.P. amended the provincial Constitution to provide for the indirect election for governor in the gubernatorial elections of 1966 in Mendoza Province. However, the Peronists split over the question of the gubernatorial candidates and presented two opposing candidates.[47] The Democrats thus elected the provincial governor and emerged as the largest party in the Provincial legislature. Afterwards, the Revolution of June, 1966, dissolved all political activity and all political parties, and—perhaps—initiated a new period in Mendocino and Argentine politics.

[46] Originally, the loyal Peronists of six different party factions were to have presented candidates in an electoral front. One week before the election, orders came from Perón that his loyal followers were to abstain from voting. After the election many of the provincial Peronist leaders felt that they had been manipulated, and they faced the problem of paying the campaign expenses.

[47] Originally, the Peronists supported the candidacy of Alberto Serú García, official candidate of the Popular Movement of Mendoza, who ranked fourth in the final vote. One faction left the M. P. M. and united with a faction of Justicialist leaders to support the candidacy of Ernesto Corvalán Nanclares, twice gubernatorial candidate for Tres Banderas and officially sponsored by Perón. Corvalán Nanclares ranked second in votes after the Democrats and stated that Serú García had previously agreed that Corvalán Nanclares was to be the candidate in 1966.

CHAPTER III

THE CERTIFICATION OF CANDIDATES

A political party's recruitment of candidates involves two distinct but complementary stages. The first stage is that of certification: the social screening and political channeling which results in the eligibility for candidacy. This stage refers to the determination by the political party of who shall be eligible for candidacy, usually upon the basis of certain requirements of social and political background. The second stage is that of selection, the actual choice of the candidates to represent the party in the general election. While certification refers to the determination of eligibility, selection refers to the designation of the actual candidates from among this group of possible pre-candidates.[1] This chapter will examine the certification of candidates.

Four functions are invariably performed by the political system of any society, however simple or complex the political institutions of that system. These four functions are: 1) political socialization of the citizenry within the elaborated political rules; 2) articulation of interests; 3) incorporation of these interests into the political system; and 4) communication.[2] Political parties are one means by which the interests, ideologies, and points of view of groups in the society are articulated and are incorporated into the political system. One method to determine what interests have been incorporated is to analyze the groups represented by the leaders of the politico-administrative elite of the political system. Because these interests can be incorporated by one government leader, part of the politico-administrative leadership, or all of the politico-administrative leadership, an analysis of the social background of the political decision makers can be used to identify the incorporation of certain interests.[3]

Students of the Argentine, in their studies of its history and politics, have generally asserted that certain political parties originated and developed as the political representatives of certain socio-economic groups

---

[1] This sense of the word "recruitment" was developed by L. C. Seligman, in his article, "Political Recruitment and Party Structure: a case study," *American Political Science Review*, 55 (1961), p. 77; and in his book, *Leadership in a New Nation*, p. 7.

[2] Gabriel Almond and James Coleman, *The Politics of Developing Areas*, p. 32. These four functions are labeled as "input" functions and are distinguished by the authors from the four "output" functions.

[3] José Luis de Imaz, *Los que mandan*, pp. 31-32.

within the Argentine society.[4] These same authors, furthermore, asserted that this representation was basically caused by the incorporation of certain socio-economic groups into the political party: the political party's membership, as well as its voting strength, was generally drawn from those particular socio-economic groups identified with it. These authors believed that it was chiefly by belonging to and acting within its own party that each socio-economic group sought and obtained political participation and representation in Argentine society. These same authors also implicitly assumed that each of these socio-economic groups tended to be characterized distinctively (and thus differentiated from one another) by certain socio-economic qualities. While few authors have stated authoritatively that each political party is associated exclusively with just a certain socio-economic group, they have agreed that each political party has tended fundamentally to represent certain socio-economic groups within the society. But these same authors have asserted that in some parties are found other—and often opposing—classes or socio-economic groups as well. For example, the Conservatives are considered to be the party of the landowning upper class, but they include some of the rural proletariat in the most rural-agricultural sections of Argentina. One frequent criticism of the Radical Civic Union has been that its membership was so heterogeneous that it either had to split or to confine itself to the most generalized political program.[5] With two exceptions these assertions have been entirely im-

[4] Bagú, *Evolución histórica de la estratificación social en la Argentina*; Ricardo M. Ortiz, *Historia económica de la Argentina*, II, pp. 169, 179, 184-185; Ciria, *Partidos y poder en la Argentina moderna*, pp. 310-311, 318; Gallo and Sigal, "La formación de los partidos políticos," *Desarrollo Económico*, III (1963), pp. 173-230; Puiggrós, *Historia crítica de los partidos políticos argentinos*, pp. 65, 89, 101, 202; Blanksten, *Perón's Argentina*, pp. 31, 267, 272, 275, 338-339; Gino Germani, *Estructura social de la Argentina*, pp. 249-260; Rubens Iscaró, *Origen y desarrollo del movimiento sindical argentino*, pp. 56-57, 81, 99, 179; Alexander, "The Emergence of Modern Political Parties in Latin America," *Politics of Change in Latin America*, p. 107; J. J. Hernández-Arregui, *La Formación de la conciencia nacional*, p. 78, 213, 291; A. R. Carranza, *Qué es la democracia cristiana*, pp. 214-215; Campobassi, *Los partidos políticos: estructura y vigencia en la Argentina*, pp. 44-49, 97-100; Olguín, *Lencinas*, pp. 55, 108, 303, 311; Campoy, "Persistencia de algunos valores sociales en una sociedad en desarrollo," and "Grupo cultural criollo bajo," p. 11; Whitaker, *Argentine Upheaval*, pp. 80-85; Cúneo, *Juan B. Justo y las luchas sociales en la Argentina*, pp. 331-332; Rennie, *The Argentine Republic*, p. 340; Galletti, *La realidad argentina en el siglo XX: la política y los partidos*, pp. 13-15, 29, 56-60, 71, 106-109, 174-179, 239; George Pendle, *Argentina*, pp. 65-66; Snow, *Argentine Radicalism*, p. 14; John J. Johnson, *Political Change in Latin America*, pp. ix, 1-2, 98, 104, 108. Marianetti, *Argentina: realidad y perspectivas*, pp. 365-377, 400, 432-433; Leopoldo Maupas, "Trascendencias políticas de la nueva ley electoral," *Revista Argentina de Ciencias Políticas*, IV (1912), pp. 420-423.

[5] See Marianetti, *Argentina:realidad y . . .*, p. 365; Leopoldo Maupas, *Revista Argentina de Ciencias Políticas*, IV (1912), pp. 420-423; Luna, *Yrigoyen*, p. 120.

pressionistic, and represent the opinions and guesses of a majority of authors, developed from their own wide reading and study of Argentine politics and society. Only two authors attempted to base their assertions upon empirical evidence or data.[6]

These students of the Argentine generally have asserted that the Conservatives consist of the creole upper class differentiated by the following characteristics: membership in certain private clubs and entrepreneurial organizations, occupations associated with the management and ownership of the means of production, higher educational level, and greater native parentage. The Radical parties consist of the immigrant middle class, differentiated by the following characteristics: membership in non-union organizations, occupations demanding professional preparation or technical skills, higher educational level, and greater immigrant parentage. The Peronist parties consist of the creole lower class, differentiated by the following characteristics: membership in unions and certain types of popular clubs, occupations demanding no professional preparation or technical skills, lower educational level, and greater native parentage. The Socialist parties consist of the immigrant lower class, differentiated by the following characteristics: membership in union organizations, occupations requiring no professional preparation (but requiring skilled laborers), lower educational level, and greater immigrant parentage. The Christian Democratic Party consists of the immigrant middle class, differentiated by the following characteristics: membership in Acción Católica, occupations demanding professional or technical skills, higher educational level, and greater immigrant parentage.

The question occurs if these assertions, which identify certain socio-economic groups with certain political parties, are applicable to the socio-economic characteristics of those parties' legislative-gubernatorial candidates, i.e., if the party selects as its candidates only those persons embodying the outstanding socio-economic characteristics of those groups in the society which have been traditionally associated with that political party. One purpose in studying the certification of candidates is to determine the extent to which the party's candidates reflect (through their own personal characteristics) the same qualities of groups within the society which the party supposedly represents. The certification

---

[6] In both instances the authors correlated the political party votes with the socio-economic characteristics (selected socio-economic variables from the census data) for the electoral area. Germani correlated political party votes with socio-economic characteristics for twenty selected precincts of the Federal Capital for the four elections of 1940, 1942, 1946, and 1948. Gallo and Sigal made a similar correlation between the political party votes in the Elections of 1912 and 1916 and the socio-economic characteristics for selected provinces in Argentina. See Germani, *Estructura social de . . .,* pp. 249-260; Gallo and Sigal, *"La formación de . . .,* pp. 198-212.

aspect of candidate selection could serve as one significant means of the articulation and incorporation into the political system of the interests, ideologies, and points of view of groups in the society. Certification could be one means of achieving the four input functions (mentioned in the introduction to this chapter) which are invariably performed by the political system of any society.

Only three empirical studies have been made of the socio-economic characteristics of either the party leadership and/or legislative gubernatorial candidates and elected representatives in the Argentine society. Gallo and Sigal concluded that significant variation existed between the party membership and the party leadership of the Radical Civic Union Party during the formative period before 1916. These authors derived their conclusion by contrasting the socio-economic background of the party's national governmental elite with an index of modernization in provinces in which a high Radical vote occurred. This index of modernization was an arithmetic value developed by the authors to measure the range of impact of certain selected socio-economic variables taken from the census data: immigration, urbanization, and literacy. These authors selected these same variables which have beeen most commonly used by students of the Argentine to associate certain socioeconomic groups with certain political parties.[7] Cantón examined only the socio-economic characteristics of national leaders upon the basis of party. He made no effort to correlate the socio-economic background of the legislators with the socio-economic background of the political parties' memberships or of Argentine society in general. Cantón presented empirical data which indicated a pronounced change in the socio-economic background of legislators during the period 1890 until 1946. This change not only demonstrated a diversification of socio-economic background but also an increasing tendency to reflect those qualities usually associated with the middle and lower classes of Argentine society. Cantón showed that this change in the types as well as the extensiveness of the legislators' social characteristics obviously coincided with the electoral success of the Radical and Peronist political movements. This coincidence was the same as the relationship between social group and political party stated in the commonly made assertions, and it thus implied that these assertions might be relevant descriptions of the certification aspect of candidate recruitment. De Imaz found a similar tendency between the governmental elite-party leadership and the political parties.[8]

One of the problems in any identification of social class is to decide upon what basis to make that identification and how to order the classi-

[7] Gallo and Sigal, *"La formación de . . .,* pp. 199-222.

[8] Darío Cantón, *El parlamento argentino en épocas de cambio: 1890, 1916 y 1946,* pp. 52-66; de Imaz, *Los que mandan,* pp. 29-44 and 184-207.

Table III-1

SOCIAL CLASS OF CANDIDATES OF DIFFERENT PARTY GROUPINGS IN
MENDOZA PROVINCE

Party groupings	Lower class	Lower middle class	Upper middle class	Upper class	Number	
Conservative	0%	26%	58%	16%	100%	(38)
Radical	4%	30%	60%	6%	100%	(101)
Peronist	12%	43%	45%	0%	100%	(68)
Socialist	19%	35%	46%	0%	100%	(26)
Christian Democrat	0%	9%	86%	5%	100%	(21)
All candidates	7%	31%	57%	5%	100%	(254)

Note: See Footnote 10 of this chapter for an examination of the method used for the classification into social status.

fication into different classes. If not an infallible guide or indicator of social class, occupation usually provides the best and sometimes one useful clue to social status in the opinion of social scientists. Generally, classifications into social classes have been upon the basis of the individual's occupation and his father's occupation.[9] Table III-1 presents

[9] Juan Meynaud, "Introduction: a general study of parliamentarians," *International Social Science Journal*, 13 (1961), p. 520. Besides the problem of deciding the basis of classification, there is also the problem of applying the system to actual cases. This author decided to use the system of classification developed by Gino Germani in his book *Estructura social de la Argentina*. Germani's system was selected because, as a study of Argentine social structure by an Argentine sociologist, it was the most pertinent. Germani determined the classification into social classes by maintaining a tight connection between the principal groups of occupations distinguished by their position within the economic system and the significance of such a position in the functioning of the economic system. The classification system used by Germani is as follows:

Upper class persons: 1) in the agricultural sector are the owners of farms or ranches of more than 2,801 acres which employ laborers or managers on these farming units; 2) in the industrial sector are the owners as well as the highest managers/directors of industrial concerns employing more than 50 persons (averaged about 200 workers and produced a gross product of 4.5 million pesos at 1946 prices—which would be multiplied by 1,000 for 1965 prices); 3) in the commercial sector are the owners of the largest wholesale and chain store enterprises; the highest managers/directors of these enterprises, banks, insurance companies, and other financial services; cabinet ministers and directors of national or provincial administrative agencies of the governmental bureaucracy.

Upper middle class persons: 1) in the agricultural sector are the owners of farms or ranches of 301 to 2,800 acres which employ laborers on these farming units; all administrators and other directive personnel of any farming units; 2) in the industrial sector the owners of industrial concerns employing between 11 and 50 workers (averaged 12 workers and produced a gross product of 140,000 pesos at 1946 prices—multiplied by 1,000 for 1965 prices); technicians or other university trained personnel of industrial concerns; 3) in the commercial sector the owners of the business establishments employing no more than seven workers (65 workers in transport, eight workers in service agencies); all professionals; technical and directive personnel in governmental services or private enterprises.

the distribution of candidates into social classes (measured by occupation only) of different ideological groups in Mendoza Province.

The great bulk (88%) of all candidates were chosen from the middle classes, and no party grouping essentially deviated from this norm, since none selected less than 80% of its own candidates from the middle classes. The party groupings, however, did show different patterns in the nomination of candidates upon the basis of social class. The Conservatives chose a majority of their candidates from the upper middle class. They were the only party grouping which chose a significant number of candidates from the upper class, although selecting one fourth of its candidates from the lower middle class. Neither the Radicals nor the Christian Democrats significantly chose candidates from either the lower or the upper classes. Both party groupings chose a majority of their candidates from the upper middle class; but only the Radicals represented the lower middle class (with a third of their candidates), while the Christian Democrats did not significantly represent this same social sector. Only the Radicals selected candidates from all social classes, which would suggest that their certification of candidates coincided with the commonly

---

Lower middle class: 1) in the agricultural sector the owners of farms of 300 acres or less as well as renters and any other form of tenancy—having no employees but dependent upon their family's labor; subordinate or junior directive personnel; 2) in the industrial sector the owners of industrial establishments employing no more than ten workers (averaged about two workers); artisans; two workers; subordinate employees in governmental service or private enterprises sector the owners of commercial or service enterprises employing no more than two workers; subordinate employees in governmental service or private entrprises.

Lower class persons: 1) in the agricultural sector the self-employed workers and permanent or temporary salaried workers; 2) in the industrial sector the industrial sector the industrial supervisors or foremen, the self-employed workers, apprentices, skilled and semi-skilled and unskilled laborers; 3) in the commercial sector the salaried and self-employed workers, and laborers. Germani's classification provided for a choice between alternative categories in many instances. For example, he classified distinguished professionals as members of the upper class. When the author was in doubt, he always classified into the lower social class category of the alternatives. This author, thus, classified all professionals as members of the upper middle class, since this author felt that his assessment of "distinguished" would have been completely subjective and since he did not include such an assessment in his questionnaire to the political party candidates.

Germani relied solely upon occupational factors as the indicators of social class. Germani did not use the system developed by Warner and other North American sociologists: that of assigning weights to selected variables (such as occupation or education or residential location), dividing the sum of these variables by the number, and thus using the quotient as the classifier into determined social class. This author used Germani's system because of its convenience and because the two obvious variables, occupation and education, generally correlated automatically. See Germani, pp. 145-146; 155-193 for the method and the discussion of the classification system; and 196-197 for a summary table of this classification system.

Table III-2

OCCUPATIONS OF CANDIDATES OF DIFFERENT PARTY GROUPINGS IN MENDOZA PROVINCE

Party groupings	Laborers	Professionals	Business-men	En-trepeneurs	Farmers and Miners	Employees	Not Classifiable	Number
Conservative	0%	50%	26%	13%	3%	3%	5%	100% (38)
Radical	3%	50%	17%	14%	6%	4%	6%	100% (101)
Peronist	7%	35%	24%	10%	6%	16%	2%	100% (68)
Socialist	15%	31%	31%	4%	0%	19%	0%	100% (26)
Christian Democrat	0%	70%	10%	0%	10%	0%	10%	100% (21)
All candidates	5%	46%	21%	11%	5%	8%	4%	100% (254)

Note: These occupational categories are the same as used by the national and provincial census for 1960 in Argentina. For a listing and discussion of these categories see Instituto de Investigaciones Económicas y Tecnológicas, *Censo nacional de población 1960*, pp. 70-71.

The category of "professional" refers to an occupation which requires either a university degree or specialized training beyond the high school, or a long apprenticeship and a special examination in order to develop certain skills. The category of "businessman" refers to persons who own enterprises which sell goods and services as well as persons who themselves sell goods and services upon a percentage basis: i.e., brokers, travelling salesmen, real estate agents, owners of drygoods stores. The category of "entrepreneurs" includes all persons who manage, administer, or oversee large productive enterprises and who may or may not own them. The category of "employees" includes all persons who occupy subsidiary positions concerned essentially with the distribution of goods and services; they form the group commonly referred to as "salaried white collar workers". For statistical purposes the separate categories of farmer and miner have been combined in this investigation.

The high number of Christian Democrats who could not be classified was due to their status as university students, who could not be classified in any employment categories. Women candidates were classified by the husbands' occupations, unless employed themselves.

made assertion, by students of the Argentine, that the Radicals are a heterogeneous political movement including all social classes. Unlike the other party groupings, however, neither the Peronists nor the Socialists had representatives from the upper class and no more than a minority from the upper middle class. Both party groupings tended to choose candidates from the lower middle and the lower social classes; but the Socialists were oriented more toward the lower class, while the Peronists were oriented toward the lower middle class.

Table III-2, indicating the occupational distribution of the candidates of different party groupings in Mendoza Province, serves as a specific presentation of types of occupations *per se* without any implications of an ordering by status or power. The professional occupations provided the largest number of all candidates as well as the largest number of candidates within each party grouping. The businessmen and entrepreneurial categories provided the second source of all candidates and, with professionals, provided two-thirds or more of the candidates for each party grouping. Different patterns emerged between party groupings, however, in the nomination of candidates upon the basis of occupations. One difference is illustrated by the fact that the Conservatives, the Radicals, and the Christian Democrats practically ignored laborers or employees in their selection of candidates. The Peronists and the Socialists, in contrast, significantly nominated one fourth or more of their candidates from these occupational sectors. While the Socialists and Peronists chose only one third or less of their candidates from the professional sector, the other three party groupings chose one half or more of their candidates from this sector. The Christian Democrats tended more to nominate candidates from the professional sector, while the Radicals tended more to nominate candidates from the businessmen-entrepreneurial sectors. Three-fourths of the Conservative candidates were professional or businessmen.

The fact that so few candidates (5%) were selected from the occupational group containing farmers might appear incongruous, since Mendoza Province has an agricultural economy based upon the growing of grapes and the production of its derivative products. But while party candidates are not directly related to agriculture by means of occupation, they are more indirectly related by other means as shown by Tables III-3, III-4, and III-5.

These Tables demonstrated that the party candidates did have a considerable indirect connection with agricultural interests and commitments. Despite the small number of directors-stockholders among all party candidates, more than a fourth of the Conservative candidates occupied such positions. The Peronists tended to ignore this type of candidate. A similar situation applied to the owners of wineries. Only the Conservative candidates included a significant number of owners;

Table III-3

STOCKHOLDER DIRECTORSHIPS OF CANDIDATES OF DIFFERENT PARTY GROUPINGS IN MENDOZA PROVINCE

Positions occupied	Total	Conservative?	Radical	Peronist	Socialist	Christian Democrat
Stockholders or directors of enterprises	15%	27%	14%	6%	11%	14%
Not stockholders or directors of enterprises	85	63	86	94	89	86
	100%	100%	100%	100%	100%	100%
Number	(254)	(38)	(101)	(68)	(26)	(21)

Note: These figures refer only to activities in provincial stock companies which were chartered by the provincial government of Mendoza. These figures were gained from an examination of 486 of the 526 stock companies chartered in Mendoza Province. The author had no means to determine the activities of Mendocinos in companies chartered by the national or other provincial governments. Practically all of the companies examined were concerned with agricultural production or the distribution of agricultural production.

Table III-4

WINERIES OWNED BY CANDIDATES OF DIFFERENT PARTY GROUPINGS IN MENDOZA PROVINCE

Ownership or wineries	Total	Conservatives	Radical	Peronist	Socialist	Christian Democrat
Owner of wineries	4%	13%	4%	0%	0%	0%
Not owners of wineries	96	87	96	100	100	100
	100%	100%	100%	100%	100%	100%
Number	(254)	(38)	(101)	(68)	(26)	(21)

Note: These figures refer only to the owners of wineries. Candidates whose fathers or other relatives owned wineries were not counted as owners of wineries.

Table III-5

LAND OWNED BY CANDIDATES OF DIFFERENT PARTY GROUPINGS IN MENDOZA PROVINCE

Ownership of land	Total	Conservatives	Radicals	Peronist	Socialist	Christian Democrat
Landowners	28%	42%	31%	19%	11%	38%
(Small landowners)	(23)	(31)	(26)	(15)	(7)	(38)
(Medium landowners)	(4)	(8)	(3)	(4)	(4)	(0)
(Large landowners)	(1)	(3)	(2)	(0)	(0)	(0)
Not landowners	72	58	69	81	89	62
	100%	100%	100%	100%	100%	100%
Number	(254)	(38)	(101)	(68)	(26)	(21)

Note: This system of classification was taken from Germani, *Estructura social de la Argentina*, p. 165. The small landowner owns up to 300 acres; the medium landowner owns between 301 and 2,800 acres; and the large landowner owns more than 2,801 acres.

very few were included among the Radical candidates; such a type of candidate was absent from among the Socialists, Peronists, and the Christian Democrats. More than a fourth of the candidates were land-owners, again with considerable variation between the parties. Almost half of the Conservative candidates were landowners, while about one-third of the Radical and Christian Democratic candidates included land-owners. The Peronists, the Socialists, and the Christian Democrats had no candidates who were large landowners, and all party groupings —except the Conservatives—had a minuscule number of large and medium landowners. Among all party groupings, the Conservatives definitely showed the strongest relationship with the agricultural-en-trepreneurial sector. They did tend to nominate as candidates persons who clearly, but indirectly, discharged these economic functions. The Radical and the Christian Democratic candidates definitely showed a weaker relationship. One of the frequent complaints by the Democratic (Conservative) leaders to the author was the unwillingness of the province's major businessmen/entrepreneurs to become involved in political activity, either as candidates or as party activists. These Democratic leaders felt that the businessman's non-involvement extended to all parties, not just to their own. While any criterion of involvement is largely a personal measurement, the above Tables show that the Democrats (Conservatives) succeeded best in attracting these desired elements into their party's political activity.

Chapter I had indicated that Mendoza Province had been settled by a mass of foreign immigrants and that this massive immigration had affected the politico-cultural environment of the province. Presumably, the results of this massive immigration would be reflected by the political parties in the certification of their candidates. Table III-6 presents the distribution of candidates of different party groupings in Mendoza Province by their place of birth. Table III-7 presents the distribution of the birthplaces of the grandfathers of candidates, while Table III-8

Table III-6

BIRTHPLACE OF CANDIDATES OF DIFFERENT PARTY GROUPINGS IN MENDOZA PROVINCE

Party grouping	Mendoza Province	Other Argentine Province	Foreign Country	Number	
Conservative	89%	7%	4%	100%	(38)
Radical	74%	22%	4%	100%	(101)
Peronist	82%	18%	0%	100%	(68)
Socialist	77%	23%	0%	100%	(26)
Christian Democrat	81%	19%	0%	100%	(21)
All candidates	79%	19%	2%	100%	(254)

Table III-7

BIRTHPLACE OF GRANDFATHERS OF CANDIDATES OF DIFFERENT PARTY
GROUPINGS IN MENDOZA PROVINCE

Party Grouping	Mendoza Province	Other Argentine Province	Foreign Country	Did not know	Number	
Conservative	13%	13%	71%	3%	100%	(38)
Radical	7%	20%	70%	3%	100%	(101)
Peronist	15%	15%	69%	1%	100%	(68)
Socialist	4%	15%	73%	8%	100%	(26)
Christian Democrat	0%	19%	81%	0%	100%	(21)
All Candidates	9%	17%	71%	3%	100%	(254)

Note: The candidates' grandfathers were examined here because of the desire for greater accuracy. Since much of the foreign immigration was in stages, many of the original foreign immigrant families would have reached Mendoza Province after the birth of children in other Argentine provinces where the family lived temporarily before continuing to its final destination. Many of the candidates' fathers, thus, would have been listed as having been born in other Argentine provinces, and thus would not demonstrate the fact that they were descended from foreign immigrant stock. Statistics about the candidates' fathers would have indicated more of an internal migration within the country rather than the extent of the original external migration from abroad.

presents the distribution by periods of arrival in Mendoza Province of the paternal families of candidates of different party groupings.

The Tables demonstrate that only a miniscule number of candidates were foreign born; the vast majority of all candidates selected by each party grouping were born in Mendoza Province. Provincial localism, thus, appeared to be one criterion for the selection of candidates by all party groupings. Yet, while themselves predominately local inhabitants, the candidates of each party grouping tended to be similar in that: 1) a majority were first generation Argentines; 2) they were predominantly drawn from families of foreign-born immigrants. The Tables portrayed a basic similarity between all party groupings in the selection of their candidates: each party grouping essentially nominated candidates from immigrant stock.

Different patterns emerged between party groupings, however, in the type of immigrant group from which candidates were nominated. Only the Conservative and Peronist party groupings still selected a significant residue of candidates from creole families. The creole candidates of the Conservatives and the Peronists, furthermore, were descended from the traditionally wealthy, landowning families originating with the Spanish Conquerers who conquered and settled Mendoza Province. Any creole candidates selected by the Radical and Socialist groups were mestizo descendents of the original Indian tribesmen who lived in the Province of Mendoza before the arrival of the Spanish Conquerers.

Another difference from the other party groupings was that one-third of the Conservative grouping's candidates were descended from

Table III-8

DATE OF IMMIGRATION TO MENDOZA PROVINCE OF PATERNAL FAMILY OF CANDIDATES OF DIFFERENT PARTY GROUPINGS IN THAT PROVINCE

Party grouping	Before 1810	From 1811 until 1889	From 1890 until 1929	From 1930 until 1962	Did not know	Number
Conservative	13%	19%	60%	5%	3%	100% (38)
Radical	2%	14%	62%	16%	6%	100% (101)
Peronist	9%	17%	61%	9%	4%	100% (68)
Socialist	4%	15%	65%	16%	0%	100% (26)
Christian Democrat	0%	15%	61%	24%	0%	100% (21)
All candidates	5%	16%	62%	13%	4%	100% (254)

Note: Families are known as creoles if they arrived to Argentina before 1810.   Immigrant families arriving after that date are known as immigrants.   The figures in the above table applied this same rule, but to Mendoza Province.   Thus, any person whose family settled in Mendoza Province after 1810 was classified as immigrant, even though his family may have originally settled in another Argentine province before 1810.

families which immigrated to Mendoza Province before 1890. The year 1890 is chosen as the decisive date because of the lack of national concern with planned immigration before that year. During the 1880's the governing Oligarchy decided to populate Argentina by means of concentrated unrestricted immigration, and 1890 marks the beginning of this immigration influx. The fact that about one-third of the Conservatives candidates' families settled in Mendoza Province before 1890 suggests the need to make a broader investigation of the general political attitudes and motivations of the Conservatives toward the various provincial governments. Families settling the Province of Mendoza before 1890 would have been able to develop their wealth and to achieve their economic positions in society by means of their own efforts, rather than as the results of any patrimony. Such families would be critical of any government which sought to regulate or in any way to interfere with that newly achieved wealth, especially a social reformer. Immigrants after 1890 would not have developed a stake or vested interest in the existing economic system, and would have tended to support a social reformer. An interesting research project would be to test this possibility by examining the socio-economic background of those who supported as compared to those who opposed reform movements. Such an investigation into the economic achievements of this earlier group of immigrants plus the marriage of many of them into the traditionally land-owning creole families might discover why some of the best known activists among the Mendocino Conservatives were immigrants or sons of immigrants.

All party groupings tended to select an equal number of candidates from families which had immigrated to Mendoza in the period 1890-1929. Candidates of the immigrant families of this period would generally be sons of immigrants. This condition could indicate that all political groups are equally open to the sons of immigrants. The condition could also indicate that a political career is associated with first-generation Argentines, as a useful means for, or the mark of, their upward social mobility and successful integration into the social system. This condition could also indicate that such a large number of candidacies by these first-generation Argentines simply reflected the aggressive displacement of the nativistic sector by the immigrant sector in Mendocino or Argentine society.

An analysis of the social background of a governmental elite generally includes an examination of the educational attainments of the members of that elite. Table III-9 presents the distribution of candidates by educational level in the different ideological groupings for Mendoza Province. In interpreting the figures of Table III-9 one should keep certain facts in mind. Although President Sarmiento initiated a public school system in Argentina in the 1880's, President Yrigoyen was considered responsible for actually implementing widespread primary edu-

Table III-9

EDUCATIONAL LEVEL OF CANDIDATES OF DIFFERENT PARTY GROUPINGS IN MENDOZA PROVINCE

Party grouping	Illiterate	Primary	Secondary	Post-secondary	University	Number
Conservative	0%	9%	28%	18%	45%	100% (38)
Radical	0%	21%	27%	14%	38%	100% (101)
Peronist	0%	24%	38%	14%	24%	100% (68)
Socialist	0%	46%	23%	8%	23%	100% (26)
Christian Democrat	0%	14%	10%	14%	62%	100% (21)
All candidates	0%	22%	28%	14%	36%	100% (254)

Note: The terms in the above table have the following meaning: "illiterate" means a person who has had no formal education; "primary" refers to persons who started and/or finished the primary school only; "secondary" refers to persons who started and/or finished the secondary school only; "post-secondary" refers to persons who began the university and/or who received specialized training beyond the high school; "university", refers to persons who were graduated from a university.

cation throughout Argentina during his first presidency from 1916-1922. It was President Perón who was considered responsible for actually implementing widespread secondary education throughout the nation. Perón is memorable, also, for the fact that he abolished tuition and other fees at state universities, of which there are now about ten for a national population of 20 million persons. These factors explain the greater significance of a university degree in Argentina, since the country has not had the tradition of widespread education at all levels in which the average citizen could easily participate. Many parts of Mendoza Province were without adequate educational facilities until after Perón. For example, the Department of Tunuyán did not have a high school until after 1958.

A high number, then, of university graduates were nominated by the party groupings, but between each party grouping there were more marked variations in educational level. The Conservatives, the Radicals, and the Christian Democrats definitely were differentiated by a higher educational level. The Peronists and Socialists, in contrast, were differentiated by a lower educational level. This marked difference between the first three party groupings and the latter two party groupings is demonstrated regardless of whether the party groupings are compared by the number of candidates with university degrees, or by the number of candidates with a secondary education or less.

An interesting facet of the educational characteristics of the candidates is the range of professional training among those having a university degree. Table III-10 shows the distribution of candidates into professionals (measured by the type of university degree) of different party groups.

The table shows that lawyers dominate among the candidates with college degrees, just as they generally do in other countries. But, more significantly, doctors formed the second largest group of professionals. The high percentage of doctors in Mendocino political parties reflects a characteristic of Latin American political parties in general.[10] There are several probable explanations for this role of the doctor. One was the intentional policy of Yrigoyen to use doctors as politicians. The very activity of the doctor brings him into constant contact with large numbers of voters and gives him greater awareness of the voters' immediate needs and concerns. Also, the nature of the doctor's activity places him in a position to perform memorable favors and to gain the respect of all voters regardless of party affiliation. Together, doctors and lawyers dominate among all the university educated candidates. One reason for the predominance of both professional types is that both discharge occupational roles in which they can perform favors for voters, in a

---

[10] De Imaz, *Los que mandan*, p. 194.

Table III-10

TYPE OF UNIVERSITY DEGREE OF COLLEGE GRADUATES AMONG CANDIDATES OF DIFFERENT PARTY GROUPINGS IN MENDOZA PROVINCE

Party grouping	Law and political science	Medicine	Economic	Physical and natural sciences	Agronomy and Veterinary	Engineering	Philosophy and letters	Number	
Conservative	47%	16%	16%	0%	0%	11%	10%	100%	(16)
Radical	57%	31%	0%	0%	4%	2%	6%	100%	(39)
Peronist	62%	19%	5%	0%	5%	0%	9%	100%	(16)
Socialist	30%	14%	14%	14%	0%	14%	14%	100%	(6)
Christian Democrat	20%	40%	20%	0%	0%	7%	13%	100%	(13)
All candidates	49%	26%	7%	2%	3%	4%	9%	100%	(90)

Note: Some candidates whose occupations placed them in higher class positions are not included because they had only specialized training beyond the high school or had not finished the university. Some pharmacists, winery chemists, procurators, and other types of legal jobs can be fulfilled by specialized training or by special examinations as well as by regular university degrees.

The term "medicine" includes dentists and pharmacists, as well as medical doctors. All are grouped together because their functions are concerned with life and health.

society characterized by the system of favors.[11] Both professions are valuable means to attract and to maintain the loyalty of party voters and followers. Oftentimes, doctors and lawyers are included upon the ballot, obviously without chances of being elected, because they are well known or are well regarded and can be exploited to attract votes in the election. Interestingly, only the Socialists had degrees in the physical and natural sciences. One explanation might be that this type of training would make them attracted to the "scientific" philosophy of Socialism.

Table III-11

RELATIONSHIP BETWEEN LABOR UNIONS AND CANDIDATES OF DIFFERENT PARTY GROUPINGS IN MENDOZA PROVINCE

Party grouping	Member of one or more labor unions	Non-member advisor of one or more labor unions	Not a member or advisor of any labor unions	Number	
Conservative	5%	0%	95%	100%	(38)
Radical	11%	2%	87%	100%	(101)
Peronist	23%	4%	73%	100%	(68)
Socialist	38%	0%	62%	100%	(26)
Christian Democrat	0%	5%	95%	100%	(21)
All candidates	15%	2%	83%	100%	(254)

Note: The term "non-member advisor" referred to a doctor or a lawyer who performed medical or legal services for the union, with or without pay. Such a person was not a member of the union.

Only 2.5% of these persons belonging to unions were related to the C. G. T., the Peronist-oriented General Federation of Labor (Confederación General del Trabajo). Nine per cent of the Peronists were members of the C. G. T., and the only non-Peronist associated with the organization was a Radical who was a non-member advisor.

Table III-11 and III-12 present the types of organizational memberships of the candidates of different party groupings in Mendoza Province. Mendocino politicians were joiners. Regardless of party grouping, the candidates had a wide network of social, occupational, or other types of organizational contacts and friendships. Both the Peronists and Socialists selected a preponderant number of their candidates from members of labor unions. Surprisingly, the Socialists nominated a greater number of labor union members than did the Peronists, despite the constitutional norm among the Peronist movement that one-third of all party candidates should be labor union members selected by the labor unions themselves. One of the constant complaints of union leaders to this author was that the present Neo-Peronists' parties in Mendoza Province had become too bourgeoise. The unionists criticized the leadership of the Tres Banderas and the Blanco Parties as being so eager to attract the middle class vote that they wanted to emphasize

[11] One politician stated to this author that the doctors allowed the voters to live, while the lawyers allowed the voters to do as they pleased.

Table III-12

TYPE OF ORGANIZATIONAL MEMBERSHIP OF CANDIDATES OF DIFFERENT PARTY GROUPINGS IN MENDOZA PROVINCE

Type of organization	Total	Conservative	Radical	Peronist	Socialist	Christian Democrat
Professional or occupational type of organization	47%	63%	55%	32%	50%	67%
Provincial stock exchange	1%	5%	1%	0%	0%	0%
Industrial Union	3%	1%	0%	0%	0%	5%
Chamber of Commerce	3%	2%	0%	0%	0%	5%
Rotary or Lions	7%	16%	9%	1%	4%	5%
El Círculo Social Club	3%	18%	0%	0%	0%	5%
Jockey Clubs	9%	18%	9%	10%	0%	5%
Gimnasia and Esgrima Social Club	16%	37%	12%	16%	0%	9%
Club Progreso	2%	0%	2%	3%	0%	0%
Andes Talleres	3%	0%	4%	4%	4%	0%
Athletic clubs	44%	37%	50%	54%	23%	19%
Acción Católica	6%	5%	3%	6%	0%	33%
Number	(254)	(38)	(101)	(68)	(26)	(21)

(Figures are partial and do not represent a total of 100%).

Note: These memberships are not exclusive of one another. Many candidates belonged to several of these organizations and thus were counted successively in the statistical information for each organizational type. The term "Jockey clubs" refers to departmental clubs, the provincial club located at the capital of Mendoza Province as well as the national club at Buenos Aires.

publically the end of the traditional association of the Peronist Movement with the popular working class. The party leaders, consequently, were fearful to include union candidates upon the parties' ballots or to assign unionists significant positions within the party hierarchy. Only the Peronists showed a definite tendency not to belong to professional or occupational type organizations. The Perón Government started these occupational organizations as a counterpart to the working class labor unions. Professionals of the same occupation were organized into an association in which the members regulated their professional activities : e.g., the amount of fees, the standards of professional conduct. Although these associations were continued after the 1955 Revolution with largely the same functions, the Peronists generally refused to participate in them as one means to voice their disapproval of the overthrow of the Perón Government.

In Mendoza Province certain social clubs traditionally have enjoyed the status of "prestige, elite" clubs in which one's membership was achieved by occupational success and wealth and which served as an indication of this achievement. While no studies have ever been made of these clubs, they do function as a common meeting ground of the socio-economico-political leaders of the province. Through their social interaction, opinions and attitudes are expressed, and—consciously or unconsciously—member politicians can become aware of consensus and dissent as regards common, public concerns. Certainly, the absence of any direct relationship of the candidates with the business-entrepreneurial organizations could be achieved informally by means of these clubs. The Gimnasia y Esgrima Club has been the best prestige and elite club. The Jockey Club has traditionally been associated with the old wealthy landowning Oligarchy, which ruled Argentina for almost a century after the 1860's. Rotary or Lions enjoy an elite status in Mendoza which they do not enjoy in the United States.

The Conservatives showed a large consistent membership among their candidates in all of these prestige clubs. The El Círculo Social Club was essentially a Conservative organization. Likewise, the Conservative candidates dominated among the candidate members of the other presigious private clubs (ranging from a mere 16% in Rotary or Lions to more than one-third in Gimnasia y Esgrima Club). The Conservative candidates tended not to belong to entrepreneurial organizations ; but their absence of any significant membership in such organizations was offset by their definite entrepreneurial role performed through corporation directorships and the ownership of land. While the Radicals and Peronists shared a significant membership in these clubs, their membership was inconsistent and generally reached about one-half of the number of the Conservative candidate members. The Radical candidates tended to join non-union organizations, although a significant number of their candidates did belong to labor unions. The Peronist candidates did tend to belong to the labor union movement, but did not belong to the popular type clubs—such as the Club Progreso or Andes Talleres—although both have been traditionally associated with the working class and Peronist Movement. In contrast to the other party groupings the Christian Democrats and the Socialists consistently showed a smaller or no membership in every organization. This condition suggests a marginal condition of these party groupings' candidates which is related to these parties' marginal condition as political and electoral movement. The Socialists tended to choose candidates belonging to the labor unions and eschewing the other types of organizational memberships, except the professional associations. The Christian Democrats did tend to choose candidates belonging to the Acción Católica as predicted and eschewing other types of organizational memberships, except for the professional associations. The large number of candidates of all parties who participated in athletic clubs consisted mostly of those candidates located in the outlying departments away from the Capital of Mendoza. In these areas the athletic club functioned as the popular social club for the area as well as merely functioning for athletic reasons.

Although students of the Argentine have generally asserted that certain political parties are associated with certain socio-economic groups in society, and although these assertions may accurately describe the outstanding socio-economic characteristics of the membership of each party grouping, these same assertions inaccurately describe the outstanding socio-economic characteristics of the candidates of each party grouping. The preceding statistical evidence demonstrated that these commonly made assertions are not valid as a completely accurate description of the peculiar representation of certain socio-economic groups in society by each political party grouping through that grouping's certification of its candidates. The reason was that fundamentally more than a majority of the candidates of any party grouping shared certain common socio-economic characteristics with the candidates of all other party groupings. Each party grouping tended generally to nominate those candidates who: 1) occupied a middle class social status; 2) worked in professional or businessman-entrepreneurial occupations; 3) were descended from immigrant stock and had foreign parentage; 4) achieved a secondary education or better, among the university graduates of which lawyers predominated.

These assertions, however, are valid as indicators of certain exaggerated biases or tendencies of each party grouping to represent certain socio-economic groups in society by means of that grouping's certification of its candidates. Although most candidates reflected a fundamentally common socio-economic background, still each party grouping demonstrated certain statistical biases in the type of individual which that grouping nominated for its candidates. The Conservatives were more oriented to nominate those candidates who: 1) belonged to the upper classes; 2) had a greater association with the management and ownership of the means of production; 3) achieved a higher educational level; 4) were more likely to be descendents of creole stock and to have native parentage; 5) belonged to certain prestigious private clubs. The Radicals best fitted the common assertion about themselves, although they were more oriented to nominate those candidates who: 1) belonged to the upper classes; and 2) were more active in business and entrepreneurial occupations. The Peronists were more oriented to nominate those candidates who: 1) belonged to the lower classes; 2) worked as employees; 3) achieved a lower educational level; 4) were more likely to be descendents of creole stock and to have native parentage; and 5) belonged to labor unions or certain prestigious private clubs. The Socialists were more oriented to nominate those candidates who: 1) belonged to the lower classes; 2) worked as employees or laborers; 3) achieved a lower educational level; 4) and belonged to labor unions. Like the Radicals, the Christian Democrats best fitted the common assertions about themselves, although they too were more oriented to nominate candidates who: 1) belonged to the upper classes; 2) belonged to professional organizations as well as Acción Católica.

CHAPTER IV

THE SELECTION OF CANDIDATES

Studies of the recruitment of political leadership have generally focused upon the social background of leaders. The study of "how," the process by which political and parliamentary leaders are selected, has been neglected.[1] This neglect has occurred despite the fact that political scientists agree that the nomination process is the most crucial and focal aspect of political parties. The nomination process is regarded as the best point from which to study political parties.[2] Recently, political scientists have increasingly focused upon the process to select legislative members. Several studies of British political parties, as well as new studies of North American political parties, have examined the process of candidate selection. Also, one study has examined candidate selection in a German political party.[3] No such investigations have been made of Latin American political parties.

One model used for the study of political parties has been Robert Michels' concept of the "iron law of oligarchy," developed from his examination of Social Democratic Party of Germany.[4] In his book, *Political Parties,* Michels concludes that all political parties become oligarchical in nature. Michels asserts that the oligarchic condition is opposite to the democratic condition. In his Preface he contends that on the continuum

---

[1] L. C. Seligman, "A Prefatory Study of Leadership Selection in Oregon," *Western Political Quarterly,* 12 (1959), p. 154; F. J. Sorauf, *Party and Representation,* p. 2; H. Jacob, "Initial Recruitment of Elected Officials in the U. S.—a Model," *Journal of Politics,* 24 (1962), p. 703.

[2] Avery Leiserson, *Parties and Politics,* p. 178; Key, *Politics, Parties and Pressure Groups,* (1958 ed.), p. 413; Seligman, "Political Recruitment and Party Structure: a case study," *American Political Science Review,* 55 (1961), p. 77; David B. Truman, "Federalism and the Party System," *Federalism: Mature and Emergent,* ed. Arthur MacMahon, p. 119; E. E. Schattschneider, *Party Government,* p. 64.

[3] Leon D. Epstein, "Candidate Selection in Britain: a comparative study," *P. R. O. D.,* II (1959), pp. 16-18; "The Selection of Parliamentary Candidates," *Political Quarterly,* 30 (1959), pp. 215-229; R. T. McKenzie, *British Political Parties,* Chapter IV and VIII; L. C. Seligman, "Political Recruitment and Party . . .," pp. 76-86; "A Prefatory Study of . . .," pp. 153-167; Sorauf, *Party and Representation;* Renate Mayntz, "Oligarchic Problems in a German Party District," in Dwaine Marvick, *Political Decision-Makers,* pp. 138-192; Austin Ranney, *Pathways to Parliament.*

[4] McKenzie used Michels' model as the basis of his study of British political parties. Another application of Michels' theory, to the deviant case of a labor union instead of a political party, was Seymour Lipset, *Union Democracy,* p. 5.

between the democratic condition and the oligarchic condition, political parties inevitably move along the continuum in the direction of oligarchy, or—having once achieved the oligarchical condition—certain internal attributes prevent the political party from moving towards the democratic condition.[5] The difficulty with Michels' theory is that he is not consistent in his use of the term "oligarchy." In effect, Michels uses five different definitions of oligarchy throughout his book and—perhaps unwittingly—changes from major reliance upon one definition to major reliance upon another definition about mid-way in his book.[6]

The most workable or testable of Michels' definitions is as follows: people who hold positions within the organization are not checked by those who hold subsidiary positions within the organization.[7] The key to this definition is freedom from control. This freedom from control means that executive's activities are unrestricted in their content or in their direction by the party membership.[8] This definition asserts that the political party's membership cannot control or veto the decisions or actions of the party's leadership. Michels demonstrates that one of the chief foci of the oligarchical leadership is in the selection of legislative candidates. Thus, according to this definition, the leadership is unrestricted by the party membership in its choice of legislative candidates. If the membership performs any role it is simply to approve formally the leadership's choice of candidates: the membership does not select the candidates nor does it effectively veto the candidates chosen and thus force the leadership to select new nominees or to accept unwanted nominees. The impotency of the membership exists despite the existence of a democratic morality within the party. The party may have been founded upon democratic principles or it may operate by democratic rules, but such principles and rules are simply a formal guise to hide an oligarchy in substance.[9] The membership is impotent because it occupies a subsidiary position. This definition and its subsequent assertion embody two of Michels' other definitions of oligarchy: 1) the minority decides; and 2) the party's leadership is the only constant source of any significant political action.[10]

This impotency of the membership exists, furthermore, whether the party's leadership is united or is divided into factions. When the party's leadership is divided into ideological factions, each faction's leaders appeal to the membership for support. Such appeals—most often in terms of the democratic morality—do not result in the membership's effective

---

[5] Michels, *Political Parties*, pp. vii-ix.

[6] C. W. Cassinelli, "The Law of Oligarchy," *American Political Science Review*, 47, (1953), pp. 778-779.

[7] *Ibid.*, p. 778.

[8] *Ibid.*, p. 779.

[9] Michels, *Political Parties*, pp. 3, 10.

[10] Cassinelli, "The Law of Oligarchy," p. 778.

participation in decisions, nor in its increased control over the leadership.[11]

The common attitude among Mendocinos has always been that the party's candidates are selected by an oligarchical party leadership. It is felt that the party leaders choose candidates upon the basis of their own selfish interest or personal whim rather than upon any consideration of the party membership's (much less the society's) interests. This method of oligarchical selection is expressed by the word "digitación," which means literally that the maximum party leader appoints the party's candidates simply by indicating them with his finger. The leader's choices are not referred to either the party membership or to the remainder of the party leadership for their approval or even for their reactions. One leader (or at most a small, restricted group of leaders) selects the candidates, and his designations are enforced vertically downward throughout the party.[12]

Traditionally, the Socialist Party has been recognized as an exception to this system of "digitación" by the leadership. From the first instance of candidate selection in 1896 until the present day the Argentine Socialists have used a system of direct election designed to assure the effective selection by the membership.[13] The present selection process

[11] Michels, *Political Parties*, pp. 164-184. In this investigation the concepts of oligarchy and democracy are differentiated upon the basis of the role of the leadership as opposed to the role of the membership (not-leadership) in decision-making within the political party. Any sharing or division of power between the elements or levels within the leadership is irrelevant to a classification as oligarchic or democratic. Thus, it is incorrect to determine the condition or extent of oligarchy upon the basis of "localism" within the party's leadership. This distinction between elements within the party leadership is sometimes mistakenly used instead of the distinction between the elements of the leadership and the membership. An example is Samuel J. Eldersveld, *Political Parties: a behavioral analysis*, pp. 8-10.

[12] Not only was this opinion common among the politically non-active public, but the author repeatedly encountered this attitude among Mendocino politicians with whom he talked.

This concept of the "digitación" of candidates is found in studies of Argentine political parties. Matienzo developed his theory of the tendency of oligarchy in Argentine political parties in his book, published in 1910 and apparently written independently of any knowledge of Michels. See Matienzo, *El gobierno representativo*, pp. 204, 237-238; Linares Quintana, *Los partidos políticos, instrumentos de gobierno*, p. 180.

[13] The party's presidential candidates are still appointed by the members of the national Executive Committee.

In the original process to select candidates in 1896, the pre-candidates were nominated by the party membership attending its own organizational meetings. Afterward a provincial-wide assembly of all party members was held to select the final candidates from among the proposed pre-candidates. See Jacinto Oddone, *Historia del socialismo argentino*, I, pp. 245, 271; Cúneo, *Juan B. Justo y las luchas sociales en la Argentina*, p. 141; Enrique Dickmann, *Los congresos socialistas*, p. 40.

essentially operates as follows: simultaneously, all party members meet
at their respective organizations; at this meeting any member may nominate any person as a candidate, after which the entire membership secretly votes between the proposed nominees; afterward, the party leaders
print a ballot containing the most voted nominees, according to the order
in which they were voted and including twice the number of nominees
as there are positions to be filled in the general election; this ballot of
pre-candidates is then mailed to each party member who (in his home)
votes for his final choices; the pre-candidates receiving the most votes
become the party's official candidates.[14] This system was designed to assure that the party membership nominated the pre-candidates as well
as finally selecting the party's candidates, to the exclusion of the party's
leadership. This method of selection was used by the Mendocino Socialist parties during the 1930's and 1940's, and it is used by the present-day
Argentine Socialist Party and the Democratic Socialist Party.[15]

In contrast to the Socialists' effort to maximize the role of the party
membership, the other parties have tended to minimize the membership's
role. Until the Revolution of 1930 the Radical parties chose their candidates by means of the convention system with all of its characteristics
so strongly criticized by Ostrogorski.[16] As a result of the Revolution of
1930 the Radical Civic Union Party amended its constitution to provide
for the selection of the party officials and party candidates by the direct
vote of the membership in internal party elections. In 1932 the Constitution of the Mendocino Radical Civic Union was amended to provide that
party officials and candidates would be elected by the system of a
direct and secret vote of the membership. Also, a system of minority
representation was provided for in the election of the party's candidates
for public office. The direct vote of the membership occurred only when
two lists of candidates were presented by opposing party factions. If
only one list was presented, then it was automatically proclaimed as

[14] These meetings are held simultaneously to prevent campaigning, pressuring,
or other forms of influence by the leadership. The Socialists feel that the system
of the postal vote prevents the development of factionalism and prevents the pre-
planning of candidacies. See *La Nación*, 6 March 1966, p. 6. The author felt that
pre-planning by party leaders or by party factions had occurred in the 1940's, but
to a very limited extent.

The system originated with Juan B. Justo, the founder of Argentine Socialism.
The author has never been able to find a bibliographic source which explicitly
explains Justo's own reasons for choosing this method of selection.

[15] In exceptional circumstances the party's provincial Congress chose the party's candidates: e.g., in 1951 at the height of the harassment by the Peronists; in
1966 when a proposed electoral coalition with the Democratic Progressives failed
just before the election. See *Carta orgánica del partido socialista argentino (1966)*,
pp. 16-20; and *Carta orgánica del partido socialista democrático*, pp. 25-33.

[16] Moisei Il Ostrogorski, *Democracy and the Organization of Political Parties*,
II, pp. 115-132.

elected. At present, the system of minority representation provides that where a faction gains at least one-fourth (25%) of the party vote of the corresponding geographical unit (i.e., the province, the electoral constituency, or the department depending upon the positions to be filled) it nominates its candidates for one-third (33%) of the ballot. However, the third position on the ballot is reserved for the first candidate of the minority, while the remainder of the minority candidates occupy the last positions upon the list. Under the Sáenz Peña Law the minority faction of a party thus could be assured of electing at least one of its own candidates; but under proportional representation, this possibility is doubtful. The success of provisions for an internal election really depends upon the existence of two or more really competitive party factions.

However, during the 1930's and the 1940's, the system of internal election was little used, since the Radical leadership consciously tried to avoid it. First, every effort was made to achieve a unified list ("lista única") of candidates by means of a compromise including the candidates of opposing party factions. Second, if creation of a compromise list failed, then the party leaders incited the provincial Congress to declare itself sovereign and accordingly to nominate the candidates. Thus, an internal election was automatically eliminated. Always at these party Congresses the procedure was for the convention president to appoint a committee of five to ten major provincial leaders to prepare a list of pre-candidates, inevitably approved by the convention delegates without discussion. Success depended upon the inclusion of a candidate from each department, who occupied an elective position upon the ballot. When disputes did occur, they generally concerned the location of candidates upon the ballot or disputes between the departmental factions as to which candidate was to be placed upon the ballot. The decision as to which candidate was to be nominated was generally made earlier by a group of five or six provincial leaders after discussions with the departmental leaders of each department.

When internal elections did occur within the Radical Civic Union, they generally were between opposing factions to decide which was to select the provincial party's officials. Rarely were there any internal elections to decide the party's candidates for public office. One explanation was the attitude that the successful selection of the party's officers also implied the right to select the party's candidates. The second reason was the fact that the Mendocino party was essentially united about party policy and party ideology. Where the factions did split because of fundamental differences, the minority faction never succeeded in attracting a strong following. During the 1930's and the 1940's the candidacies were essentially selected by an oligarchical party leadership.

Never during the 1930's nor the 1940's did the membership of the Democratic Party itself participate in the selection of the party's candidates. The national legislative and gubernatorial candidates were chosen by the party's provincial convention, while the provincial legislative candidates were chosen by the party's constituency conventions. These conventions were well-ordered, disciplined, and brief meetings in which the conventional delegates obviously ratified *pro forma* the candidates selected by the party leadership. A small group of leaders decided the party's candidacies as well as all party affairs.

Democratic candidates whom the author interviewed were unanimous that party decisions were made by a small group of the provincial leaders, ranging in size from three to six persons. While they agreed that the party was very undemocratically managed during the 1930's, they feel that—in general—the party now suffers from too much democracy. Candidates of other parties always cited the Democratic Party of this period as the pure example of an oligarchically managed, provincially centralized party.

When disputes did occur, they were between factions of the provincial or the departmental leadership: then the decisions were made by the leadership without the participation of the membership. Only once did the membership participate in an internal election, and that was in the election of party officials during the height of the dispute between factions during the 1930's. It was characteristic of the Democratic Party that its candidates were selected by the pure form of oligarchy.

Within the Peronist Party the party leadership selected all candidates, without the participation of the party membership. Although candidate selection within the party may be divided into two periods, the difference between them concerned the role of provincial party leadership versus the national party leadership in the selection of candidates. This change will be discussed in the following chapter.

The selection process within the Mendocino parties may be divided into several stages preceding the general election. Although artificial and arbitrary, this division is perhaps the most useful means to demonstrate the method of candidate selection. Each stage is inter-dependent upon the other; each stage may follow one another consecutively, or various stages may occur simultaneously. Also, one candidacy may start at a different stage or may omit a certain stage. Although each process of selection will depend upon each individual candidacy, enough similarity exists to make this divisional system useful.[17] In a condition of pure oligarchy each stage would be entirely performed by the party leader-

---

[17] Suggested sources for these stages are: Epstein, "Candidate Selection in Britain: . . .," pp. 16-18; Sorauf, *Party and Representation*; L. C. Seligman, "Political Recruitment and . . .," pp. 77-86; "A Prefatory Study of . . .," pp. 153-167; "Recruitment in Politics," *P.R.O.D.*, I (1958), pp. 14-17; Mayntz, "Oligarchic Problems in . . .," pp. 138-192; V. O. Key, *Southern Politics*, pp. 410-413; Leiserson, *Parties and Politics*, pp. 100-104, 178-180.

ship without any participation of the party membership or non-party groups.

Preparatory to the actual selection is the enlistment of members and, among them, of potential leaders into the party. In a condition of pure oligarchy there would be a conscious effort by the party leadership to enlist potential leaders upon the basis of some rational and qualitative criteria, as a means to perpetuate the position of the already existing oligarchy. Otherwise the supply of new members would be more and more haphazard and on the basis of personal initiative for irrational reasons.

Table IV-1 depicts the sources of enlistment into membership of the candidates, while Table IV-2 indicates the reason why candidates joined their own party. Among all party groupings approximately three-fourths or more of the candidates became party members upon their own initiative, while the leadership never initiated more than one-fifth of the party membership of the candidates. The enlistment of members was not dominated by the party leadership; there was no conscious effort by the leadership to recruit new party members as a means to maintain itself in power. But neither was this stage dominated by the party membership or by the pressure groups (not-leadership). Rather the enlistment stage was characteristically a haphazard situation, determined essentially by the particular action of the newly entering members himself. The not-leadership then could participate, but chose not to do so.

Except for the Conservatives and the Peronists a great majority of candidates joined their party because of belief in or attraction by the party's program. The largest number of Conservatives joined their party because of environmental factors: family heritage or association with friends who were Conservatives. While these environmental factors were also significant for the Radicals, they were much less important than for the Conservatives. The largest number of Peronists joined their party because it had the best electoral possibility, either in terms of its vote getting ability or of its legal recognition. A surprising demonstration of Table IV-2 was the insignificant number of all candidates, as well as any party grouping's candidates, who joined because of their belief in or attraction by the party's national leader. Chapter I mentioned the importance of charisma in the political style practiced by the Argentines. One would expect that this motivation would be important among Peronists, since the movement is still relatively young and since its original founder is still alive. The founders or original idols of Radicalism, Conservatism, or Socialism have long since died. Probably this motivation was stronger among the Peronists and explains why only the Peronists had such a large proportion of candidates who chose their particular party because it had electoral possibilities. Participation in a party which is legally recognized or is electorally strong would allow these followers

Table IV-1

INITIATION OF PARTY MEMBERSHIP OF CANDIDATES WITHIN DIFFERENT PARTY GROUPINGS IN MENDOZA PROVINCE

Party grouping	Candidate's own initiative	Initiative of a party member, not a leader	Initiative of a party leader	Did not know	Never member of party for which a candidate	Number
Conservative	87%	0%	13%	0%	0%	100% (38)
Radical	83%	0%	15%	0%	2%	100% (101)
Peronist	78%	0%	16%	0%	6%	100% (68)
Socialist	81%	8%	11%	0%	0%	100% (26)
Christian Democrat	71%	0%	19%	10%	0%	100% (21)
All candidates	81%	1%	15%	1%	2%	100% (254)

Note: This figure of 10% of "did not know" among the Christian Democrats refers to candidates who were enlisted for party membership, but they did not know by whom.

Recruitment of Candidates in Mendoza Province

Table IV-2

REASON FOR MEMBERSHIP OF CANDIDATES WITHIN DIFFERENT PARTY GROUPINGS IN MENDOZA PROVINCE

Reason of membership	Total	Conservative	Radical	Peronist	Socialist	Christian Democrat
Belief or attraction of national leader	5%	3%	8%	6%	0%	0%
Environment of family or friends	11	29	13	7	0	0
Belief in party program	48	32	58	25	69	77
Best party: people, organization	10	16	8	12	8	9
Frustration within other party	5	2	4	12	0	0
Opposition to government or activity of opposing party	6	18	3	0	4	14
Party with electoral possibility	10	0	0	36	0	0
Party which defends class interests	4	0	4	2	15	0
Other	1	0	2	0	4	0
Number	100% (254)	100% (38)	100% (101)	100% (68)	100% (26)	100% (21)

Note: Only the first reason mentioned by the respondent during the interview was recorded. Each candidate is thus listed only once in the above statistics.

These statistics should be read with some reserve. Oftentimes this investigator felt that the candidates tended to respond in that manner which they felt the investigator would want to hear. The responses, consequently, tended to be too idealistic, since they felt that the investigator would have responded in this manner himself. The investigator felt that many more responses would have been in the categories of "belief in a national leader" or "environment of family or friends".

Irrational reasons would include just these categories: "belief in a national leader" or "environment of family or friends". All other categories would be classified as rational.

to fulfill the aspirations of their leader. The remainder of the candidates in each party grouping showed a wide variation as to the reasons they joined their party. Only a significant number of candidates joined Socialism because it defended class interests. Only the Peronists had a significant number of candidates who joined because of frustration within another party. Most of these candidates were members of the Justicialist Party, the continuation of the original Peronist party, who had quit the Radical movement because of frustration with that party's leadership. Both a significant number of Conservatives and Peronists felt that their's was the best party, either in quality of the leadership, internal organization or process. Significantly, a quantity of Conservatives or Christian Democrats entered their parties because of opposition to the government or activity of the opposing political party. Most of these candidates were motivated by a reaction against what they felt was the totalitarian nature of the Perón Government from 1946 until 1955 and of its subsequent political movements.

Both Tables indicated that personal initiative, generally for rational reasons of the individual member, dominated as the source of party membership. Any deliberate or successfully deliberate effort by the party leadership to enlist new members, and potential leaders consequently, was absent. Only the Christian Democrats demonstrated a proportionately higher number of candidates who joined their party upon the initiative of others. A probable explanation is that its condition as a new movement just establishing itself, forced the leadership to recruit new members actively and aggressively. Enlistment of new potential members by a party leadership tends, at best, to be haphazard and certainly not for the purpose of getting potential leaders as a means of oligarchical self-perpetuation.

The first stage in the selection of a candidate is that of pre-planning, where party elements examine the possible candidacies among themselves and with one another. In this stage opinions are exchanged, and the cases for favorite candidates are presented, examined, and then disregarded or accepted. Consensus or disagreement develops around suggested candidacies, and factionalism commences to organize itself. This pre-planning may occur among the leadership, the membership, or pressure groups. In the condition of a pure oligarchy, the party leadership is very active in pre-planning in order to perpetuate itself in power.[18] This situation of pre-planning is illustrated by Table IV-3, showing the candidate's perception of the origin of his own candidacy.

Overall, the role of the party membership in the pre-planning of candidates is limited. Simultaneously, the Table indicates a fundamental

[18] Mayntz, "Oligarchic Problems in . . .," pp. 154-157; V. O. Key, *Politics, Parties and Pressure Groups* (1958), pp. 411-413; Michels, *Political Parties*, p. 177.

Table IV-3

SOURCES OF PRE-PLANNING OF CANDIDACIES WITHIN DIFFERENT PARTY GROUPINGS IN MENDOZA PROVINCE

Party grouping	Party membership	Labor Union leadership	Party leadership and membership or labor union leadership	Party leadership	Number
Conservative	3%	0%	0%	97%	100% (38)
Radical	1%	0%	1%	98%	100% (101)
Peronist	0%	7%	3%	90%	100% (68)
Socialist	100%	0%	0%	0%	100% (26)
Christian Democrat	0%	0%	10%	90%	100% (21)
All candidates	11%	1%	3%	85%	100% (254)

Note: In this Table only the governor was included within the category of party leadership for the Conservatives. The reason was that 10% of the Democratic (Conservative) candidates were chosen by the provincial governor.

Together the party membership and the labor union leadership form the category of the "not-leadership" in order to distinguish them from the political party leadership.

difference between the different parties which is to be a recurring characteristic of the selection process in Mendocino political parties: the control and management of the selection process by the party membership within the Socialist parties. The party membership is the origin of all candidacies in the Socialist parties. This unanimous response by the Socialist candidates did not mean that the party members themselves performed the stage of pre-planning through the discussion of possible candidacies and arranging to support a list of candidates by bargaining. Before 1946 there were sporadic efforts at such pre-planning; but this limited practice seems to have disappeared completely at the present time. The Socialist responses simply indicated that there was no definite stage of pre-planning. Among the other parties the non-leadership elements participated significantly only within the Peronist and Christian Democratic parties. The labor union officials performed this role within the Peronist parties, either exclusively or in co-operation with the party leadership—in keeping with the party officials' practice of granting specific representation to labor union organizations. The only significant role of a party membership was in the Christian Democratic Party, a non-elective party, and then the participation was shared with the party leadership. Almost all candidacies originated with the party leadership. If the party leadership did not monopolize the pre-planning of candidacies, it controlled it to such an extent that it functioned as a monopoly in the practical sense. The greater role of the not-leadership is explained essentially by the inclusion of the Socialists in the statistics. Elimination of the Socialists would reduce the role of the party membership to an insignificant level.

Instigation is closely related to pre-planning and is the urging or the persuading of a person to accept a candidacy. Instigation is the matching of a candidate with the sponsorship initiated by the pre-planning. Table IV-4 indicates who solicited the candidates, while Table IV-5 suggests the reasons for solicitation within the Mendocino party groupings. With the exception of the Socialists, the party leadership within all other party groupings instigated the candidacies to the practical exclusion of the not-leadership elements. Only in one case did the actual party membership itself instigate a candidacy. In the other three cases of instigation by the not-leadership sources, the instigation was made by labor union officials—instances in which the performance of this function was specifically assigned to non-party elements by the party leadership.[19] Many labor union officials felt that within the Neo-Peronist parties the labor unions' share of the candidacies had tended to diminish or to disappear altogether. During the Perón government, in contrast, the party

[19] Sorauf found that among Pennsylvania candidates non-party sources instigated a little more than 20% of the candidacies, contrasted to only 3% among Mendocino parties. See Sorauf, *Party and . . .*, pp. 101-102.

Table IV-4

SOLICITATION OF CANDIDATES WITHIN PARTY GROUPINGS IN MENDOZA PROVINCE

Party grouping	Not-leadership only	Shared by not-leadership and party leadership	Party leadership only	Not solicited	Number	
Conservative	0%	3%	89%	8%	100%	(38)
Radical	1%	2%	92%	5%	100%	(101)
Peronist	4%	4%	82%	10%	100%	(68)
Socialist	0%	0%	0%	100%	100%	(26)
Christian Democrat	0%	5%	71%	24%	100%	(21)
All candidates	2%	3%	77%	18%	100%	(254)

Note: The term "not-leadership" refers to the party membership and/or the labor union leadership.

Table IV-5

REASON FOR SOLICITATION OF CANDIDACY WITHIN PARTY GROUPINGS IN MENDOZA PROVINCE

Reason solicited	Total	Conservative	Radical	Peronist	Socialist	Christian Democrat
Personal friendship	2%	0%	3%	2%	8%	0%
Party position, activity, seniority	28	32	24	37	23	19
To fill ballot	7	3	9	4	0	19
Personal capacity	23	32	26	16	15	19
Factional candidate	12	10	13	16	0	9
Attract votes	10	10	7	9	4	5
To balance ticket	7	10	0	7	0	5
Family name	1	3	1	2	0	5
Representative of a pressure group	2	0	0	7	4	0
Did not know	8	0	4	0	46	19
Number	100% (254)	100% (38)	100% (101)	100% (68)	100% (26)	100% (21)

Note: Only the first reason mentioned by the respondent in the interview was recorded. Each candidate is thus listed only once in the above statistics.

had awarded one-third of the candidacies to the labor union sector for
its selection. In six cases the party leadership shared the instigation
with the not-leadership. Again two of these cases were with the labor
union leadership. Instigation, then, was the party leadership's function
and intentionally assigned to or shared with non-party elements only
in rare cases. Within the Socialists instigation was not a function of the
party leadership. Elimination of the Socialists from Table IV-4 would
have made the statistical role of the party leadership even higher.

One characteristic of Mendocino political parties is that the candidate
does not himself initiate his own candidacy. The "self-starter" does
not characterize Mendocino political parties.[20] In Mendocino political
culture the rule states that each candidate is solicited or requested to
serve as a candidate. Even if this solicitation is only a mere formality
to hide a candidate's initiation of his own candidacy, it must still be
observed. Major party leaders, thus, who have already arranged their
nominations with other party leaders, still observe the ceremony of a
delegation of party notables and party friends visiting the future nominee
and humbly requesting that the leader serve his party and his fellow-
Mendocinos by accepting the proferred candidacy.

The Socialists do not have this rule and do not observe the solicitation ceremony. The Socialists regard efforts at pre-arranging any candidacy to be unconstitutional if attempted by party leaders and unethical
if attempted by party members. The Socialists regard candidacies as originating spontaneously from among the membership at the organizational nominating meetings. The unsolicited Peronist, Democratic, Radical candidates were usually nominated for a candidacy without their
knowledge. This author interviewed ten candidates who had not known
of their nomination and inclusion upon the election ballot until told by
the author. The other unsolicited candidates were nominated and then
notified of their selection, generally just before the deadline to submit
the list of candidates in order to intensify the pressure of the nominee
to sign the list without any hesitation. A significant number of Christian
Democratic candidates were not solicited generally because they were
the major or only party leaders in areas where the party was unorganized
or weakly organized.

The candidates were chosen for three types of reasons, two of which
were more important in the selection process. The major type of reasons
was organizational in nature: the candidate's participation and relationship within the party organization, party activity, party position and
office, and party seniority. This reason was the dominant one or an

---

[20] This concept of the "self-starter" originated with Seligman and referred to
the candidate who instigated his own candidacy or whose candidacy was instigated
by non-party groups. See Seligman, "A Prefatory Study of Leadership Selection
in Oregon," *Western Political Quarterly*, 12 (1959), pp. 162-163.

equally important one within all party groupings. The second major type of reasons was technical in nature: the individual's capacities, preparation or ability, or previous experience and reputation. While the chief cause for solicitation within the Peronists, it was an equally important one for all other party groupings. The third type of reasons varied in type and in significance among all party groupings. Factional causes referred to the creation of a ticket which would achieve the support of all party elements: candidacies representing certain factions; inclusion of unopposed or non-controversial candidates. Interestingly, this cause was significant only among the elective party movements in Mendoza Province: the Conservatives, the Radicals, and the Peronists. Similarly, the desire to attract votes was significant only among the elective party movements: the Conservatives, the Radicals, and the Peronists. The term "to balance the ticket" referred to the need to represent party elements which were not structured factionally: inclusion of women, geographical or ideological representation. This reason was significant only for the Conservatives, the actual government provincially. The need for representation of pressure groups was strongest with the Peronists, but not to a significant degree. Apparently the insignificance of this reason reflected the decreased role of the labor union movement within the Peronist party grouping. The number of candidates who did not know or could not guess the reason for their candidacy was significant only within the Socialists and the Christian Democrats. Probably, their condition as non-elective movements plus the Socialists' norm against the solicitation ceremony explains this condition. Among all party groupings ascriptive factors, such as personal friendship or family name, were insignificant reasons in the instigation of candidacies.

Presentation follows instigation; it is the stage where the individual is presented within the party as a sponsored pre-candidate. Presentation does not refer to the formal nomination by the party of its electoral candidates, but it refers to each of several proposals as a pre-candidate within any of several party organs. Table IV-6 indicates the sources of this initial sponsorship of a candidate, while Table IV-7 shows the party organ in which this initial sponsorship occurred within the various party groupings in Mendoza Province.

The party leadership practically monopolized the presentation of candidates within the Conservatives, Radicals, Peronists, and Christian Democrats. Only within the Socialist parties did the membership monopolize the presentation of pre-candidates. In all other party groupings, the membership may have been present and may have participated in the presentation meeting, but the party membership did not effectively serve as a source of sponsorship. The cases of seven Peronist candidates were distinct: the pre-candidates were either presented by the labor union officials or by the union officials and the party leadership combined. In

Table IV-6

SOURCES PRESENTING CANDIDATES FOR FIRST TIME WITHIN PARTY GROUPINGS IN MENDOZA PROVINCE

Party grouping	Not-leadership only	Shared by not-leadership and party leadership	Party leadership only	Did not know	Number
Conservative	0%	0%	100%	0%	100% (38)
Radical	0%	0%	98%	2%	100% (101)
Peronist	6%	4%	90%	0%	100% (68)
Socialist	92%	0%	0%	8%	100% (26)
Christian Democrat	0%	0%	95%	5%	100% (21)
All candidates	11%	2%	85%	2%	100% (254)

Note: The category "not-leadership" refers to party membership and/or the labor union leadership. Within this category 9% of all candidates, or 92% of the Socialist candidates, were initially presented by the party membership. Two per cent of all candidates, or 6% of the Peronist candidates, were initially presented by the labor union leadership. The category of "shared" refers to candidates presented jointly by the labor union leadership and the party leadership.

Table IV-7

TYPE OF PARTY ORGANIZATION IN WHICH CANDIDATES PRESENTED FOR FIRST TIME WITHIN PARTY GROUPINGS IN MENDOZA PROVINCE

Type of organization	Total 2%	Conservative 0%	Radical 0%	Peronist 6%	Socialist 0%	Christian Democrat 0%
Labor Unions	15	0	8	1	73	24
Departmental meeting of the party membership and the party leadership	46	66	54	56	0	33
Departmental meeting of the leadership only	2	0	2	3	0	5
District Convention	19	24	28	9	0	19
Provincial committee	11	8	6	25	0	5
Provincial Executive Committee	1	2	0	0	0	5
Provincial Convention		0	2	0	0	9
Did not know	4				27	
Number	100% (254)	100% (38)	100% (101)	100% (68)	100% (26)	100% (21)

Note: Convention or committee representatives and delegates would be included within the leadership category.

Table IV-8

TYPES OF SUPPORT BY PARTY MEMBERSHIP FOR CANDIDATES WITHIN DIFFERENT PARTY GROUPINGS IN MENDOZA PROVINCE

Party grouping	No perception of support by party membership	Covert support	Membership petitioned or spoke to leadership in favor of candidacy	Membership spoke, voted in favor of candidacy	Did not know	Number
Conservative	95%	0%	0%	5%	0%	100% (38)
Radical	65%	0%	2%	31%	2%	100% (101)
Peronist	87%	0%	2%	11%	0%	100% (68)
Socialist	0%	0%	0%	100%	0%	100% (26)
Christian Democrat	76%	0%	0%	14%	10%	100% (21)
All candidates	70%	0%	1.5%	27.5%	1%	100% (254)

Table IV-9

CANDIDACIES DECIDED BY PARTY PRIMARY WITHIN PARTY GROUPINGS
IN MENDOZA PROVINCE

Party grouping	Candidacies decided by party primary	Candidacies not decided by party primary	Number	
Conservative	5%	95%	100%	(38)
Radical	17%	83%	100%	(101)
Peronist	5%	95%	100%	(68)
Socialist	100%	0%	100%	(26)
Christian Democrat	0%	100%	100%	(21)
All candidates	19%	81%	100%	(254)

all cases the party membership did not serve as the source of sponsorship. The party membership did participate significantly in the presentation meeting, apparently more as a source of opinion and assessment. But such significant membership participation occurred only within the Socialists, as expected and where the participation by the leaders would only have been in the role of members, and within the Christian Democrats, the other non-elective party. The Radicals were the only other party grouping in which the membership's participation approached the level of significance.

The fourth stage is that of screening. Screening refers to the efforts, immediately following the first presentation, to garner support for a potential pre-candidate or to develop opposition against other pre-candidates. At this stage there tends to be factional agreements and trades, as well as efforts by the party leadership to obtain the withdrawal of pre-candidates. Support or opposition might be open: where a party element publically declares its support or opposition to a pre-candidate, works in favor or in opposition to a pre-candidacy, or presents its own sponsored pre-candidate in opposition. Covert support or opposition occurs when a party element works quietly and distributes its resources without publicity, or when a faction agrees to support a pre-candidate it originally opposed. No support or opposition refers to the passivity of a party element regarding a particular candidacy.[21] Table IV-8 through IV-10 indicate the extent and the roles of the party membership in the screening of the parties' candidates.

Interpretation of these Tables becomes more meaningful by keeping in mind the percentage of candidates selected by the party membership in a party primary. The party membership participated in the screening process in approximately three of every ten candidacies. Among these three, it was able to vote or to approve candidates in a meaningful or decisive manner—by means of an internal party election—in only two candidacies. This formal vote or approval by the party membership,

[21] These terms were suggested by Sorauf, *Party and . . .*, pp. 53-58.

Table IV-10

TYPES OF OPPOSITION BY PARTY MEMBERSHIP TO CANDIDATES WITHIN DIFFERENT PARTY GROUPINGS IN MENDOZA
PROVINCE

Party grouping	No perception of opposition by party membership	Covert opposition	Membership voted against candidacy	Did not know	Number
Conservative	100%	0%	0%	0%	100% (38)
Radical	84%	0%	14%	2%	100% (101)
Peronist	94%	0%	6%	0%	100% (68)
Socialist	61%	0%	39%	0%	100% (26)
Christian Democrat	91%	0%	0%	9%	100% (21)
All candidates	87%	0%	11%	2%	100% (254)

furthermore, occurred to a significant degree only among the Socialists or the Radicals. Within the Socialist parties any role by the leadership during the screening stage in candidate selection was effectively bypassed. The system of nomination and mail vote developed by the Socialists was designed specifically to exclude any role by the leadership, with its formation of supporting coalitions through bargaining and concessions among the leadership. Only within the Popular Radical Civic Union was the party membership able to participate in a party primary to determine the candidacies, but this participation was confined almost entirely to formal voting: expressing approval or disapproval of a factional leadership's earlier choices.

Within all other political parties the membership could not express formally its vote or approval of the candidacies, or was able to express it only to an insignificant degree. Where the party membership was able to participate in the screening stage (only one out of every ten candidacies), the party membership was limited to the informal expression of its opinion. In these cases the party leadership was free to accept or to reject the membership's view-point. This informal expression of opinion, furthermore, occurred significantly only within the Radicals, Peronists, and the Christian Democrats.

Except for the Socialists and the Popular Radical Civic Union parties, the party leadership generally and effectively managed (or was able to manage) the screening of all candidacies without any significant participation by the party membership. Except for the Socialists and the Popular Radical Civic Union parties, the screening stage generally served as just one more instance of candidate selection by an oligarchical party leadership. Part of the membership's general insignificance was probably due to the fact that it could only be consulted by means of the veto, which would tend to support Michels' conclusion about the physical impossibility of truly democratic decision-making by the party membership collectivity.[22]

The discrepancy between the percentage of candidates selected by a party primary and the number of candidates who received a favorable membership vote requires some explanation. One cause was the form of the membership's vote: another was the quality of the candidates' perception. Generally, in the non-elective parties, the candidates were first nominated in departmental and district meetings in which the party membership as well as the party leadership participated.

Non-elective parties were those parties which had not and could not hope to elect their gubernatorial-legislative candidates: Movement for Integration and Development, Intransigent Radical Civic Union, Christian Democrat, and Democratic Socialist.

In many cases the membership did participate in the discussion and

[22] Michels, *Political Parties*, pp. 26-67.

the formation of opinion in support of or in opposition to certain pre-candidacies within these parties. In these instances the membership was used in a screening capacity but only at the tolerance of the leadership. The other cause was the quality of the membership's participation. Some candidates tended to classify approval by the provincial party convention or departmental meetings as examples of membership participation. Although incorrect, this tendency was probably unintentional and easily explainable. As one descends the leadership hierarchy, the distinction between the condition of a mere party member or a mere party leader becomes more blurred, especially with the non-elective parties such as the Christian Democrats. In these cases there is no practical distinction between a titled party position and the condition as a party member. The other factor is that many candidates felt the party leadership adequately and accurately reflected the membership's attitudes. When party leaders met and decided, consequently, this situation was automatically considered as a meeting and a decision by the membership. The differences between the figures concerning membership support and membership opposition stem from the general reluctance of the candidates to give information which did not present their candidacy in the best possible circumstances.

The decisive stage is that of the binding nomination or selection. The significant characteristic of any party's nomination is:

> ". . . whether or not it is binding, whether it effectively commits the whole party to support it . . . (The) test is does it bind?"[23]

Oftentimes the formal nomination is not the same as the binding nomination. For example, the formal nomination may be by the provincial convention of a party, while the effective and binding nomination was already made by the provincial committee of party leaders (since their decision is always automatically ratified by the party's provincial convention). Most concerns and discussions of oligarchy versus democracy in a political party have focused upon this stage. When this stage is dominated and controlled by the leadership by means of the caucus or the convention system of nomination, then the party is considered oligarchic. In contrast, the party primary or internal party election is considered a means to democratic control by the membership.[24]

Only the Socialist parties provide for the system of automatic primaries. Three of the parties (Popular Union, Blanco, and Christian Democrat) used the system of the provincial or district convention for the nomination of candidates. With all other parties, the party primary is optional. The Constitutional provisions of the political parties (ex-

---

[23] E. E. Schattschneider, *Party Government*, p. 64.

[24] Sorauf, *Political Parties in the American System*, p. 51; Key, *Politics, Parties and . . .*, p. 408; Leiserson, *Parties and Politics*, pp. 243, 103.

cepting those previously mentioned) which relate to the selection of candidates are largely concerned with regulating these internal party elections. However, all Constitutions provide that the primary is to be used only where two or more opposing lists of candidates are presented. When only one list of candidates ("lista única") is presented, it is automatically proclaimed as elected without any primary. The primary system of the Socialist and Radical parties has already been examined. The Democrats' primary is decided by a simple plurality; the majority lists gets only two-thirds of the candidacies if the minority achieves 50% of the votes obtained by the majority. If no list of pre-candidates is presented, then the party's provincial convention can select all candidates; or the provincial convention can dispense with the constitutional rules and empower the provincial committee to decide. The M. P. M. and Justicialists (Peronist) Parties also provide for the primary if necessary. Both parties allow the minority to obtain one-third of the candidates upon the ballot if the minority achieves 25% the party vote. The minority would, however, obtain the last positions upon the ballot, useless elective positions under the system of proportional representation. This situation would not encourage factional conflict.

These internal party primaries are convoked and are managed entirely by the party leaders themselves. Such a condition could, of course, increase the oligarchical tendencies within a party. There are no national nor provincial laws which require internal party elections. National law requires only that the democratic system is to be observed within the internal party process.[25] No guidelines are provided as to what is the democratic system or how it is to be implanted by this legislation. In Mendocino parties the overwhelming desire of the party leaders is to avoid an internal election by achieving one unified list of candidates which represents all party elements or which leaves such a weak opposition that an election obviously becomes useless. The party primary is not mandatory in Mendocino parties and certainly is not wanted by the leadership.

Table IV-11 depicts this stage of the binding nomination in Mendocino parties by presenting the candidate's perception of that particular action in the selection process which effectively caused all party elements to accept their nomination as decisive. This Table does not necessarily depict the ultimate, formal nomination step in the selection process.

Within the Socialists the party membership effectively nominated the candidates, to the exclusion of the party leadership. Within all other parties the candidates perceived the party leadership and not the party

---

[25] See *Estatutos de los partidos políticos, (1964), Ley 16, 652*, p. 2. Sorauf, in his investigation of the selection of Pennsylvania state legislators, found that the party leadership effectively determined the choice of the party's candidates—despite state primary laws.

Table IV-11

TYPES OF BINDING NOMINATION OF CANDIDATES WITHIN PARTY GROUPINGS IN MENDOZA PROVINCE

Party grouping	Selection by labor union leadership	Selection by province-wide party primary	Selection by district or departmental party primary	Selection by party leadership	Did not know	Number
Conservative	0%	0%	5%	95%	0%	100% (38)
Radical	0%	15%	2%	82%	1%	100% (101)
Peronist	5%	0%	5%	90%	0%	100% (69)
Socialist	0%	100%	0%	0%	0%	100% (26)
Christian Democrat	0%	0%	0%	91%	9%	100% (21)
All candidates	1%	16%	3%	78%	2%	100% (254)

membership as the authoritative selector of candidates. The party leadership imposed its choices in eight out of every ten cases, and the non-leadership elements selected only two among every ten candidates. Within the latter elements the labor union leadership chose three candidates for the Peronists which meant that another organizational leadership simply replaced the party organization's leadership in the selection function. It was only within the Popular Radical Civic Union Party that the party membership itself significantly participated at the stage of the binding nomination. The membership performed a minor role in authoritatively selecting candidates within the Democrats (only two candidates) and Peronists (only three candidates of the Popular Movement of Mendoza).

Yet, this participation by the membership was in the form of voting: expressing approval or disapproval between candidates already selected by the party leadership. The form of the membership's participation in the selection process, in effect, was that of an arbitrator between two sets of candidates previously chosen by the leadership. In these instances, although the party membership was participating in the selection of candidates, its participation was effectively limited to choosing between two alternative slates of candidates. This situation poses the question of the practical effects of a party primary upon the party oligarchy and whether a party primary can be merely more than a *pro forma* ratification of the oligarchical leadership's previous decisions?

The party leadership is overwhelmingly successful in its desires and efforts to avoid the party primary. There are several reasons for this reluctance to hold a party primary in the selection of candidates within Mendocino parties. One reason is the traditional idea that an internal party election to choose party officials also serves as a nomination primary: whichever faction wins the leadership positions, automatically has the privilege to select the candidates for the forthcoming general election. In several instances a province-wide or departmental internal election to determine party officers had preceded the entire process of candidate selection and thus served as a type of pre-primary. Another reason is the leadership's dislike of the party primary as a disruptive factor, creating internal antagonisms and divisions which continue long after the primary is over. Perhaps the most important reason is the time, expense, and general strain on party leaders in creating and maintaining a winning coalition for the primary. Much of the time of party leaders is spent in getting new members to join the party so that they can vote in the forthcoming party primary, as well as arranging for the transportation of voters and the general campaigning. One factor which is decisive in any election is finances. No study has been made of national or provincial election campaign costs in Argentina. However, the author did obtain some tidbits of information which indicated that wealthy party leaders were the usual source of income for a party primary. It was estimated that one party primary in 1964 cost over three million pesos: the winning faction spent more than two million (one million of which was contributed by the provincial leader of this faction) ; the losing faction spent one million, which was borne by its provincial leaders. This estimate does not include the contributions in the form of gasoline, printing, and other activities which were performed by governmental agencies. One factor in the selection of party leaders, at the provincial and at the departmental levels, in Mendocino parties is their ability to contribute lavishly (or to have access to such contributions) to the election costs. This dependence upon the wealthy party leaders for party finances could, of course, very well be a factor increasing the oligarchical tendencies within the political party.

Two causes explain why internal party primaries did occur in the selection of candidates within Mendocino parties. One cause was constitutional: the Socialists observed the party primary, because it was obligatory by both Socialist parties' constitutional requirements. Immediately before the 1966 general election the leadership of the Argentine Socialist Party chose the candidates after the provincial party Congress agreed to dispense with the required party primary. The justification was the need to select a list of candidates quickly, after efforts to form an electoral front with the Progressive Democrats failed just before the election. Similar situations, where the party leadership selected the candidates for an electoral front with another party, had characterized the Socialists during the 1930's but had become rare since then. Within the Socialists the party style and the party myth system resulted in the authoritative selection of candidates by the party membership. Habitual acceptance by the party membership combined with habitual implementation by the party leadership meant that the membership's authoritative selection of candidates was regarded as one of the basic "rules of the game," as a fundamental tenet in the party's "way of doing things."

In the other cases factionalism was the reason for the internal party primaries. Within the Popular Radical Civic Union two strong factions existed, neither of which was willing to accept the other faction's proposals to form a unified list ("lista única").

Before the 1965 general election the provincial leaders of the Popular Cause Faction and the Recuperation Faction met and attempted to form a unified list. The Recuperation Faction demanded that all candidates be shared 50%-50% between the two factions and that a special Provincial Committee be formed under the chairmanship of the Recuperation Faction's choice. The Popular Cause Faction proposed that in the electoral districts won by each faction in the 1964 internal party election, the winning faction would choose two-thirds of the candidates and the losing faction would choose one-third of the candidates. The Popular Faction, thus, would have chosen the majority of the candidates. The efforts failed, because neither faction was willing to modify its original proposals. In 1965, before the 1966 general election, the two factions' leaders met and tried again to form a unified list. These efforts failed when the Recuperation Faction's leaders refused to accept the Popular Cause's pre-candidate for governor. As with all the Socialists, almost all of these Radical candidates were chosen in province-wide or district-wide elections, thus allowing the entire party membership the right to express its preference. The Democratic and Peronist candidates were chosen in departmental elections. All resulted from factional disputes in which certain leaders refused to accept one unified list of candidates, formulated by provincial and departmental leaders as a compromise in order to avoid a primary. After the primary election within the Democratic Party, the leaders of the winning faction agreed to replace one of their own candidates by the first candidate of the losing faction. The purpose was to insure the party's unity. In effect, the party leadership ignored the decision of the party membership as expressed through the internal party primary. The membership's participation within the Socialist parties, in contrast, was unrelated to internal party factionalism.

One of the assertions made by Michels was that factionalism within a political party does not result in the membership's effective participation in the selection of candidates. Although the factional leadership may appeal for the membership's active support, and although this appeal may be made in terms of democratic morality, this action by the leadership does not result in the membership's effective participation in the selection of the candidates. Michels asserted that the party membership is just as excluded and just as passive in the decision-making process during and after factionalism as before the internal factionalism. The evidence disproves the inevitability of this assertion by Michels. Factionalism within the Democrat, the Popular Radical Civic Union, and the Popular Movement of Mendoza did cause the factional leadership to appeal to the membership for support. Factionalism did cause the party membership's effective participation as the definitive arbitrator in the selection process. The limited extent of the membership's participation was caused by the limited and temporary extent of internal party factionalism. Factionalism ended in the Popular Radical Civic Union because of the failure of the Recuperation Faction to maintain a substantial party following among the party membership. Although losing the internal party election in 1965, the factional leadership still refused to quit the party in order to operate independently. Likewise, the factional Democratic leadership of the First Electoral District agreed within itself not to use further any party primaries. The party primary within the Popular Movement of Mendoza occurred within the Department of Godoy Cruz because of the refusal of one leader to accept a compromise list of candidates and his own personal attitude that party primaries should be used as the best means to insure a democratic process internally. In these instances the decisions of elements of the party leadership to appeal to the party membership did result in the membership's participation. In these instances the membership's participation ended with the leadership's decision to avoid this alternative means to settle disputes (as with the Democrats or the Peronists) or with the inability of the leadership to continue with the alternative method (as with the Radicals). In these parties the membership's participation was dependent upon the intensity and the durability of factionalism within the leadership.

The ultimate step in the selection process is the location of the candidate upon the party's ballot for the general election. The common assumption is that the system of proportional representation reinforces a party's oligarchical leadership.[26] In Mendocino parties, when the party primary is used, the internal election itself determines the candidate's location upon the ballot. The number of votes received in the internal election by mail determines the candidates' position upon the ballot within the Socialist parties. Within the Radical parties the minority faction gets the third candidacy upon the ballot if it wins 25% of the vote. In the Democratic and Peronist parties the losing factions get the ultimate positions upon the ballot, actually the un-elective positions under the present system of proportional representation as well as the former system of the Sáenz Peña Law. When, however, there is no party primary, the party must have some other source of decisions as to location on the ballot. Table IV-12 shows this source, while Table IV-13 shows the reason as to ballot location.

The party leadership completely or effectively monopolized the decision as to the candidates' ballot location within the Conservative, Peronist, and Christian Democrat party groupings. Only within the Socialists and the Radicals did the party membership effectively decide the candidates' ballot location; the party membership monopolized this decision within the Socialists and shared it significantly only among the Popular Radical Civic Union Party. There was no significant joint decision-making between the party leadership and the not-leadership elements within any other party. Within the Peronists these joint decisions were made between the party leadership and the labor union leadership. It is interesting to note that, while the labor union officials actively participated to a greater extent in the other stages of the candidates' selection within the Peronists, they were largely excluded from this stage of deciding the position upon the ballot. The attitude that the membership and the leadership together decided the ballot position was found specifically in the M.I.D. Party. The leadership of the M.I.D.

---

[26] Maurice Duverger, *Political Parties*, pp. 151-152.

Table IV-12

ELEMENTS DECIDING CANDIDATES' BALLOT POSITION WITHIN DIFFERENT PARTY GROUPINGS IN MENDOZA PROVINCE

Party grouping	Party membership	Party leadership with the not-leadership	Party leadership only	Did not know	Number
Conservative	0%	0%	100%	0%	100% (38)
Radical	17%	2%	79%	2%	100% (101)
Peronist	0%	3%	97%	0%	100% (68)
Socialist	100%	0%	0%	0%	100% (26)
Christian Democrat	0%	2%	88%	10%	100% (21)
All candidates	17%	1%	81%	1%	100% (254)

Table IV-13

REASON FOR CANDIDATES' LOCATION UPON BALLOT WITHIN DIFFERENT PARTY GROUPINGS IN MENDOZA PROVINCE

Reason for ballot location	Total	Conservative	Radical	Peronist	Socialist	Christian Democrat
Party primary	10%	0%	0%	0%	100%	0%
Candidate requested this position himself	11	10	17	7	0	5
Personal capacity	4	3	7	2	0	5
Candidate's party position or seniority	19	23	20	21	0	14
Relationship to pressure group	2	0	0	6	0	0
Leadership's decision	12	29	12	4	0	24
To fill ballot	6	3	7	10	0	5
Importance of department	15	21	16	18	0	5
Factional agreement, balance, or lack of opposition	16	11	12	32	0	14
Did not know	5	0	9	0	0	28
Number	100% (254)	100% (38)	100% (101)	100% (68)	100% (26)	100% (21)

Note: The statistics for the category "party primary" refer only to the Socialist candidates. Although some Peronist and Democratic candidates were the result of an internal party election, these candidates' ballot position was decided by the party leadership either after the election or before the election. The 17 candidates of the Popular Radical Civic Union were placed upon the ballot for the general election according to the results of the party primary. They are, however, classified in this Table according to the original reasons for which they were located upon the factional ballot previous to the internal party election.

had decided to allow the candidates themselves to determine their own ballot position in order to avoid the provincial leaders' involvement in frictional disputes. This condition, however, was statistically insignificant since most of the M.I.D. candidates themselves were departmental party leaders and thus were counted in the leadership category. Removal of the Socialists would have made the participation by the not-leadership elements nil.

The candidate's "political weight" was the dominant factor in determining the candidate's location upon the ballot. The term "political weight" refers to a party leader's power that he can exert to achieve his goals because of his condition or situation within the party. Political weight would include such factors as the political debts that a politician can command in return for past favors, the authoritative party position occupied, the utility of representing a bloc of party members or a geographical segment of the party, or factional support or opposition to the candidacy. Political weight determined one-half or more of the candidacies within the elective party groupings: the Conservatives, the Radicals, and the Peronists. In Mendocino parties a candidate's political weight due to his party position or to the importance of his department was most decisive among the Conservatives and the Radicals. Other conditions such as factionalism, balancing the ticket to represent all party elements, the situation of the candidacy evoking no opposition, or the need to represent non-party organizations, were determining factors among the Peronists and the Christian Democrats. Factors of personal capacity or representation of pressure groups were insignificant among all party groupings, in contrast to their greater significance among all groupings in the solicitation stage of the nomination process. Location because of the candidates' own personal requests or because of the need to fill the ballot was significant only among the Conservatives, the Radicals, and the Peronists. The high number of "don't knows" among the Christian Democrats was probably explained by their grouping's condition as a non-elective movement. The absence of total variation among the Socialists' responses indicates the deeply instilled party norms regarding the party primary.

CHAPTER V

DECENTRALIZATION OF MENDOCINO PARTIES

In his book Michels also asserted that in political parties having two or more levels of leadership, the lower level of leadership is concerned with suppression of external threats to its power position and to its self-preservation stemming from the higher level of leadership. Within a political party encompassing differing geographical areas the party leadership of each area is in constant struggle with the other; the lower level constantly seeks freedom from control by the higher level of leadership. The oligarchy at the level of the state, the province, or the commune seeks independence from any external authority or direction. Michels concluded, however, that these tendencies toward decentralization within a political party are merely the replacement of one centralized oligarchy by many localized oligarchies. Within its own region these localized oligarchies become equally as centralized and as resistant to any efforts at decentralization by internally lower levels of leadership within the same region.[1] Michels made this assertion about international parties (the national leadership versus the international leadership) and about national parties (the provincial leadership versus the national leadership). Although Michels failed to state definitely whether this condition would also apply to provincial parties (county or departmental leadership versus provincial leadership) as well as to state exactly how this decentralization would affect the factor of the selection of candidates, one could assume certain assertions by projecting Michels theory. He asserted that each level of the party's leadership selects the party's candidates corresponding to that geographical level. Thus, the county or departmental party leadership selects the candidates at the county or departmental level.

Michels regarded federalism as a variable regulating the extent of the oligarchy, but not affecting the essential nature of the oligarchy, within the political party process. Michels is asserting the inevitable existence of the condition of "localism" so characteristic of North American political parties.[2] Many North American political scientists would

---

[1] Michels, *Political Parties*, pp. 196-201.

[2] North American political scientists classify political parties in the United States as decentralized political parties, wherein the Congressional candidates are selected without centralized control or direction by the national party leadership. In contrast, political scientists have classified European political parties as centralized, where the selection of parliamentary candidates is centrally controlled or directed by the national party leadership. See Leiserson, *Parties and Politics,*

agree with Michels that federalism is a major cause of decentralized parties. Other factors, such as the presidential form of government and staggered elections, are generally cited as re-inforcing this influence of federalism.[3]

A study of the Argentine political parties is especially relevent since certain institutional and historical similarities exist between the political systems of Argentina and the United States which would tend to suggest a similarity in party decentralization. First, as the United States has done, the Argentine Constitution has provided for the federal system as the basis upon which to organize the nation. Second, Argentina uses the presidential form of government and a system of staggered elections. However, Argentine scholars generally agree that this constitutional federalism is theoretical and symbolic rather than actual. As previously explained in Chapter I, Argentine scholars feel that national centralization and control has replaced provincial autonomy—essentially by presidential manipulation of the intervention power. This characteristic of national centralization is applied to the nation's political parties as well as to the governmental system.[4]

However, some political parties, such as the Radical and the Socialist parties have always asserted their belief in the federal form of organization: internally for its party organization, as well as externally for the national organization. One of the basic ideological tenets of Radicalism has always been its strong belief in federalism and local autonomy, internally within the party, as well as externally in the national govern-

pp. 195-197; J. M. Burns, *Congress on Trial*, p. 39; David Truman, "Federalism and the Party System," in Arthur MacMahon, *Federalism: Mature and Emergent*, pp. 119, 122; E. D. Schattschneider, *Party Government*, pp. 99-106; E. P. Herring, *The Politics of Democracy*, pp. 23-24; V. O. Key, *Politics, Parties and Pressure Groups*, (1958), p. 335; Sorauf, *Party and Representation*, pp. 1-2; Truman, *The Governmental Process*, pp. 278-279; Duverger, *Political Parties*, pp. 53, 60; R. T. McKenzie, *British Political Parties*, pp. 219-220, 277.

However, Ranney's recent study of British political parties demonstrates that "localism" in candidate selection is equally characteristic of the Labour and Conservative Parties. See Austin Ranney, *Pathways to Parliament*, pp. 272-274, 281.

[3] Leiserson, *Parties and Politics*, p. 197; Schattschneider, *Party Government*, pp. 123-129; Ranney and Willmoore Kendall, *Democracy and the American Party System*, pp. 494-499; Key, *Politics, Parties and . . .*, p. 358; Truman, "Federalism and the . . .," pp. 119-121; and *The Governmental Process*, pp. 278-279.

[4] Busey, *Latin America*, p. 150; Zorraquín Becú, *El federalismo argentino*, pp. 248-249, 270-271; Blanksten, *Peron's Argentina*, p. 146; Gómez, *Argentine Federalism: its theory and practice*, pp. 186, 192-193, 252-260; C. H. Haring, "Federalism in Latin America," in Christensen, *Evolution of Latin American Government*, p. 341; A. F. Macdonald, *Government of the Argentine Republic*, pp. 152, 156-157, 169; Rowe, *Federal System of the Argentine Republic*, pp. 4, 9; W. S. Stokes, "The Centralized Federal Republics of Latin America," in *Essays in Federalism*, pp. 100-101; Vítolo, "Intervencionismo del Estado," *Cuadernos de Proceso*, I (1952), p. 26; Matienzo, *El gobierno representativo*, p. 200.

ment. In party platforms the Radicals have always emphasized their opposition to any central, national authority in favor of the provincial and municipal authority. To prevent national centralization and to insure provincial autonomy, the authors of the party's constitution consciously organized the party upon the structure of the North American political parties. Efforts by Yrigoyen to control the selection of the Radical's gubernatorial candidates failed, and even during his 1928-1930 Intervention in Mendoza Province the evidence suggests that national leaders acted more as arbitrators instead of as dictators in the selection of candidates.[5] During the 1930's and the 1940's the national Radical leaders did not intervene in provincial affairs, and candidates were decided by the provincial party leadership. The original constitution of the Socialist party was written by its founder, Juan B. Justo, to assure a system of complete decentralization: not only within the national party, but within the provincial parties as well. The Democratic Party of Mendoza has always considered itself an independent provincial party which directs the national organization of the provincial conservative parties. The only time that national leaders intervened within the Democratic Party was in the 1930's during the dispute between internal party factions, and then the only role of the national leadership was as a "friend of the court" in an effort to help settle this dispute. Traditionally, the Socialist, Radical, and Conservative parties of Mendoza Province have been free of national control and direction of the nomination process.

Candidate selection within the Peronist Party may be divided into two periods: the period before 1949 and the period after 1949. The periods were different as regards the role of the national party leadership in the selection process. The Peronist movement originated as an electoral coalition between the Labor Party and the Radical Civic Union Council of Renovation. In both parties, the candidates were selected by the provincial and departmental leaders by means of factional discussions and agreements: national party leaders did not participate in these nominations. Partly because of the inability of these two separate parties to co-operate harmoniously, and partly because of Perón's own concept of political leadership,[6] these two parties were forcibly fused into the

---

[5] *Los Andes,* 6 August 1930, p. 5; 16 August 1930, p. 3; 18 August 1930, p. 3; 19 August 1930, p. 3; 21 August 1930, p. 3.

[6] Perón's theory of political leadership was as follows: 1.) the contemporary technological developments enable, as well as necessitate, a nationally centralized political leadership; 2.) a political party's leadership may be divided into two levels: the national leadership and the regional-local leaderships; 3.) the role of the national leadership is to make the fundamental programmatic decisions for the entire country; 4.) the role of the regional-local leadership is to implement and to administer these decisions according to the conditions of the particular locali-

Peronist Party— managed and controlled centrally by the national leadership of the Superior Council in Buenos Aires. The candidates were chosen proportionally within the party, and the final selection was made by the national party organization. After 1949 this system of proportional representation meant that one third of the candidates was chosen by each of the following sectors of the party: the labor union sector, the male (political) sector, and the female sector. Each sector of the Mendocino party recommended its nominees for provincial legislators and indicated its feeling about proposed gubernatorial and national legislative candidates to its respective national leadership.

Whether this national selection was the actual effective decision or whether it was merely a formal approval is hard to determine. It would appear that the national party leadership actually decided the candidacies for national legislators and for the provincial governorship, while the provincial and departmental party leaders indicated their opinions as regards these particular candidacies and actually selected the candidates for provincial legislators. A majority of the Peronist political actors of that period, whom the author interviewed, expressed this distinction in candidate selection. The final list of all candidates was transmitted through the provincial interventor (the provincial parties were always intervened to assure national control and direction) from the National Superior Council. Despite the common attitude of the rigid structural character of the Peronist Party, this author was impressed by the seemingly organized anarchy of the movement. This author suggests that while the national leadership guarded its right of final approval, it also carefully noted the intensity of feeling and the political weight of every faction within the provincial party in the selection of candidates. Thus, the national leadership operated more as an amicable "broker" and final arbiter between disputing factions within the Mendocino Party. The provincial interventor performed this function at the provincial level in the selection of candidates for provincial legislators. Such a system would fit into Perón's theory of the informational flow upward within the party.[7] Candidate selection within the Peronist Party was nationally centralized for certain candidacies and provincially centralized for certain other candidacies.

Tres Banderas, founded in Mendoza Province in 1961, was the

---

ty or region. See Juan Perón, *Conducción política*, pp. 41-42, 100-103; *Organización peronista*, pp. 335-336.

Perón had effective supreme authority of the Peronist Party and exercised unlimited control of all party organs at all levels. See Blanksten, *Perón's Argentina*, p. 336. It is interesting to note that while Perón wrote a book about the function, the organization, the training and preparation, and the necessary qualities of political leadership, he never indicated how that leadership was to be recruited.

[7] See Perón, *Conducción política*, p. 100.

first Neo-Peronist party in Argentina which participated in the election after the 1955 Revolution. Tres Banderas accepted the ideology of Perón but rejected any leadership by him or by his party representatives in Buenos Aires. The M.P.M. was a fusion in 1963 in Mendoza of the Tres Banderas and Blanco Parties, upon the same principles.

Furthermore, Argentina, as the United States, has had the historical experience of strong sectionalism and of the need to resolve a relationship between the autonomous provincial and local authority and central national authority.[8] Sectionalism has been a characteristic of Mendoza Province. Mendocinos have traditionally had a strong regional spirit, which would, of course, encourage provincial independence. The reasons for the strong sectionalism of Mendocinos have been caused by her distinctive immigration from Chile, as well as by the political history of the provincial political parties.[9] In conclusion, certain historico-institutional factors would encourage party decentralization, despite the general feeling of students of the Argentine that its political parties are centralized. Mendoza Province would be an ideal laboratory to test this condition of centralization because of its tradition of strong regionalism and party autonomy.

These assertions by Michels about the inevitable development of geographical decentralization within the political party were tested in two ways. The first test was of a generalized nature while the second test was more specific. First, all candidates were asked how they perceived the intervention, during the selection process, of higher levels of party leadership in the geographically lower levels of party organization. Also, the candidates were asked to assess the effectiveness or the ineffectiveness of this intervention. Afterward, each stage of the process of the selection of candidates was examined to determine both the extent and the effectiveness of the participation by each level of the party leadership in the nomination process.

Table V-1 through V-4 measure the candidates' perception of intervention by the national party leadership in the selection of candidates within the different party groupings in Mendoza Province. Table V-1 illustrates the extent of this intervention. Table V-2 suggests the reason for the intervention policy. Table V-3 depicts the method of intervention. Table V-4 indicates the effectiveness of this intervention.

The Conservative, the Socialist, and the Christian Democratic candidates perceived of their own parties as free of national direction or intervention by the national leadership in the selection of candidates within

[8] Ricardo Levene, *A History of Argentina*, pp. 352-358; Romero, *A History of Argentine Political Thought*, pp. 59-126; Matienzo, *El gobierno representativo*, p. 341; Stokes, "The Centralized Federal . . .," pp. 96-99.

[9] See Gabriel del Mazo, *El radicalismo*, I, pp. 11-12, 46-51; Alfredo Galletti, *La política y los partidos*, pp. 35-38; Cesar Barros Hurtado, *Hacia una democracia orgánica*, p. 38; Cúneo, *Juan B. Justo y las luchas sociales en la Argentina*, p. 140.

Table V-1

INTERVENTION BY THE NATIONAL PARTY LEADERS IN THE SELECTION
OF CANDIDATES WITHIN DIFFERENT PARTY GROUPINGS IN MENDOZA
PROVINCE

Party grouping	Rare situation of intervention in the provincial party	Common situation of intervention in the provincial party	Did not know	Number	
Conservative	100%	0%	0%	100%	(38)
Radical	83%	17%	0%	100%	(101)
Peronist	85%	15%	0%	100%	(68)
Socialist	100%	0%	0%	100%	(26)
Christian Democrat	95%	0%	5%	100%	(21)
All candidates	88%	11%	1%	100%	(254)

---

the Mendocino parties. Although a small minority within their respective groupings, still a significant number of Radicals and Peronists perceived of intervention by the national party leadership as a common occurrence within their own parties. Interestingly enough, there was an equality and similarity of perception between the two groups despite the heritage of national centralization within the Peronists. In both groupings the reasons for this intervention were factional: the desire of the national leadership to maintain its factional strength within the provincial party or the desire of the provincial factions to obtain the support and aid of the national leaders. Only in a very few instances did the national leadership intervene to preserve factional balance or equality. The methods of intervention by the national party leadership within these two groups was clearly related to factional conflict. The Radical and Peronist national leaders mostly limited themselves to those methods related to the aiding and the furthering of their faction's efforts: the expression of opinion or the active support of a certain candidacy. Only in a very few instances did the national leader actually choose the candidates.

The effectiveness of this intervention by the national leaders within these two groups, furthermore, depended upon the existence and the extent of this provincial factionalism. National intervention was effective only to the extent that it was supported or tolerated by a provincial faction or factions. Where the provincial leadership was united and/or opposed to control or direction by the national leaders, efforts at national intervention failed. Only among the Peronists did the national leaders select provincial nominees despite provincial opposition. The smallness of the figures was surprising in view of the extent of national centralization of the Peronist Party during the Perón Government, and it simply served as an indication of the extent to which the contemporary Neo-Peronist movements were independent. The other figure of interest was the significant number of Radicals who saw a change from previous

Table V-2

REASON FOR INTERVENTION POLICY OF THE NATIONAL PARTY LEADERS IN THE SELECTION OF CANDIDATES WITHIN DIFFERENT PARTY GROUPINGS IN MENDOZA PROVINCE

Reason for intervention policy	*Total*	*Conservative*	*Radical*	*Peronist*	*Socialist*	*Christian Democrat*
Only stated that intervention occurred	4%	3%	14%	0%	0%	0%
Intervened to further factional interests	10	0	14	17	0	0
Intervened to maintain factional balance	.5	0	3	0	0	0
Intervened to assure ballot location	.5	0	3	0	0	0
Complete autonomy of the provincial leadership	59	94	38	77	39	43
Prohibited by the Constitution or party norms, morality	12	0	8	1	61	28
Other reasons for no intervention	9	0	17	5	0	14
Did not know or did not answer	5	3	3	0	0	15
Number	100% (254)	100% (38)	100% (68)	100% (101)	100% (26)	100% (21)

Note: Only the respondent's first answer was recorded; thus, each candidate is classified only once in the above statistical analysis.

"Other reasons" consisted of such explanations as: the absence of internal disputes, the national leadership not knowing the candidates, no electoral chance for the party, would disrupt party unity. None of these reasons was significant enough, by itself, to be listed separately.

Table V-3

METHOD OF NATIONAL PARTY LEADERS TO INTERVENE IN THE SELECTION OF CANDIDATES WITHIN DIFFERENT PARTY GROUPINGS IN MENDOZA PROVINCE

Party grouping	National leaders choose provincial candidates	National leaders express opinions to provincial leadership	National leaders aid certain candidacies	National leaders intervene to select provincial level candidates	Did not answer	Not applicable	Number
Conservative	0%	0%	0%	0%	0%	100%	100% (38)
Radical	8%	5%	11%	4%	6%	66%	100% (101)
Peronist	7%	7%	2%	0%	7%	77%	100% (68)
Socialist	0%	0%	0%	0%	0%	100%	100% (26)
Christian Democrat	0%	0%	0%	0%	9%	91%	100% (21)
All candidates	5%	4%	5%	2%	5%	79%	100% (254)

Note: The term "provincial level candidates" includes all candidates for national deputy or provincial gubernatorial positions.

Table V-4

EFFECTIVENESS OF INTERVENTION BY NATIONAL PARTY LEADERSHIP IN THE SELECTION OF CANDIDATES WITHIN DIFFERENT PARTY GROUPINGS IN MENDOZA PROVINCE

Effectiveness of intervention	Total	Conservative	Radical	Peronist	Socialist	Christian Democrat
National leaders effective despite provincial opposition	1%	0%	0%	4%	0%	0%
National leaders effective since supported by group of provincial leaders	8	0	16	7	0	0
National leaders ineffective if opposed by provincial leaders	7	0	13	10	0	0
Previously, national leaders selected; now, autonomy of provincial leaders	5	0	12	0	0	0
Did not know	6	0	10	4	0	10
Not applicable, did not perceive of intervention by national leaders	73	100	49	75	100	90
	100%	100%	100%	100%	100%	100%
Number	(254)	(38)	(101)	(68)	(26)	(21)

national intervention to present-day provincial autonomy. These responses were made by candidates and former members of the Intransigent Radical Civic Union, who felt that national intervention in the selection of candidates had been characteristic of the party during the Frondizi Government. But with the Revolt of 1962, the split of the party into two separate parties under Frondizi and Alende, and the increasing condition of the Intransigents as an electoral minority, meant that the provincial party was ignored by the national leadership in the selection of candidates.

Mendoza Province has always been the stronghold of the Conservative Movement. Rather than being the object of intervention, the Mendocino leadership has always considered itself to be the manipulator of the national leadership. This condition was illustrated by the almost unanimous agreement among the Conservative candidates who regarded provincial autonomy (provincial strength vís-a-vís national strength) as the explanation of non-intervention by the national leadership. A similarly high level of agreement among the Peronist candidates that provincial autonomy was the safeguard against national intervention indicated again the strength of the Neo-Peronist Movement, which began in Mendoza Province. The Socialists and Christian Democrats, likewise, regarded provincial autonomy as one restraint against national intervention. But both groups' candidates, and especially the Socialists, regarded the party's customs and morality as the more decisive restraint against national direction and control. All the Democrats and almost all the Radicals and Peronists ignored this factor of party Constitution and morality.

Mendocino politicians, generally, did not perceive of their provincial political parties as being more closely articulated with the national party leadership. Almost all would have asserted that the national party leadership was ineffective in controlling the lower provincial levels of the party; a similar assertion was made by Michels. The Tables showed, furthermore, that not only were Mendocine political parties regarded as decentralized nationally, but also that Mendocine politicians did not regard the national party leadership as always seriously attempting to intervene and to direct the party at the provincial or lower levels. The statistical evidence, especially, would challenge Michels' assertion that the national party leadership was constantly trying to control and to direct the provincial party.[10]

This investigation was concerned to determine not only whether the candidates perceived of national party centralization, but whether or not they perceived of a similar condition of provincial party centralization. Provincial centralization, in this case, would be the intervention of the higher level provincial party leadership in the selection of

[10] Michels, *Political Parties*, pp. 196-201.

Table V-5

INTERVENTION BY THE PROVINCIAL PARTY LEADERS IN THE SELECTION
OF CANDIDATES WITHIN DIFFERENT PARTY GROUPINGS IN MENDOZA
PROVINCE

Party grouping	Rare situation of intervention in the departmental party	Common situation of intervention in the departmental party	Did not know or answer	Number
Conservative	44%	53%	3%	100% (38)
Radical	41%	47%	12%	100% (101)
Peronist	46%	53%	1%	100% (68)
Socialist	100%	0%	0%	100% (26)
Christian Democrat	86%	5%	9%	100% (21)
All candidates	53%	41%	6%	100% (254)

candidates within the lower level departmental party. Table V-5 through V-8 measure the candidates' perceptions of intervention by the provincial party leadership in the selection of candidates within the different party groupings in Mendoza Province. Table V-5 illustrates the extent of this intervention. Table V-6 suggests the reason for this intervention policy. Table V-7 depicts the method of intervention. Table V-8 indicates the effectiveness of this intervention.

Within the Conservative, Radical, and Peronist party groupings intervention by the provincial party leadership was regarded as a more common occurrence. Half or more of the candidates of these groupings perceived of provincial intervention as a common practice, while the perception of similar intervention by the national leaders never achieved the figure of 20%. In contrast, to this characteristic of provincial intervention within the elective party groupings, all or almost all of the candidates of the non-elective party groupings failed to perceive a similar characteristic within their own parties.

Causes for this practice of intervention by the provincial party leadership varied between each party grouping. Nearly half of the Conservative candidates named this desire to get "qualified" candidates, or "technicians", as the reason for intervention. This concern to insure the selection of technically qualified candidates, as well as politically qualified candidates, has always been a principle of the Conservative's provincial leadership in Mendoza Province. Traditionally, the Democratic Party's provincial leadership has reserved the first candidacy for provincial deputy and for provincial senator from each district to be filled with its own choice of candidate. Under the Sáenz Peña Electoral Law, the provincial leadership generally reserved the first few places on the ballot from each district. The term "few" was flexible and could be expanded or contracted according to the particular circumstances. The provincial leadership selected more candidates because both the depart-

Table V-6

REASON FOR THE INTERVENTION POLICY OF PROVINCIAL PARTY LEADERS IN THE SELECTION OF CANDIDATES WITHIN DIFFERENT PARTY GROUPINGS IN MENDOZA PROVINCE

Reason for intervention policy	*Total*	*Conservative*	*Radical*	*Peronist*	*Socialist*	*Christian Democrat*
Intervened to obtain moral or capable candidates	18%	47%	13%	18%	0%	9%
Intervened to obtain their choice of candidates	12	18	13	16	0	0
Intervened to further their faction's interest	12	3	21	16	0	0
Intervened to maintain the factional balance	2	3	1	4	0	0
Intervened for other reasons	6	8	7	9	0	14
Complete autonomy of the departmental leadership	14	3	10	12	12	28
Prohibited by Constitution or party norms and morality	13		1	7	80	25
Previous consultation between departmental and provincial leaderships	7	9	10	6	0	5
Provincial leaders uninterested, desire to avoid conflicts or no elective chance of party	8	3	10	10	8	9
Did not know or answer	8	3	14	2	0	10
Number	100% (254)	100% (38)	100% (101)	100% (68)	100% (26)	100% (21)

Note: Only the respondent's first answer was recorded; thus, each candidate is classified only once in the above statistical analysis.
The category of "other reasons" consisted of such explanation as: intervention only to assure the candidates' location upon the ballot in an elective position or intervention because the departmental party was unstructured and the provincial leaders needed to perform this function.

Table V-7

METHOD OF THE PROVINCIAL LEADERS TO INTERVENE IN THE SELECTION OF CANDIDATES WITHIN DIFFERENT PARTY GROUPINGS IN MENDOZA PROVINCE

Party grouping	Prov. leaders choose dept. candidates	Prov. leaders express opinions to dept. leaders	Prov. leaders veto candidates selected by dept.	Prov. leaders initiate a counter candidacy	Prov. leaders arrange unwanted candidate in a non-elective place	Did not know	Not applicable	Number
Conservative	5%	59%	5%	3%	5%	5%	18%	100% (38)
Radical	2%	25%	15%	7%	6%	10%	35%	100% (101)
Peronist	19%	26%	6%	3%	6%	6%	34%	100% (68)
Socialist	0%	0%	0%	0%	0%	0%	100%	100% (26)
Christian Democrat	5%	9%	0%	0%	0%	5%	81%	100% (21)
All candidates	7%	27%	7%	4%	5%	7%	43%	100% (254)

Table V-8

EFFECTIVENESS OF INTERVENTION BY PROVINCIAL LEADERS IN THE SELECTION OF CANDIDATES WITHIN DIFFERENT PARTY GROUPINGS IN MENDOZA PROVINCE

Effectiveness of intervention	*Total*	*Conservative*	*Radical*	*Peronist*	*Socialist*	*Christian Democrat*
	13%	26%	17%	9%	0%	5%
Provincial leaders effective despite dept. opposition	18	21	22	24	0	0
Provincial leaders effective since supported by group of departmental leaders	6	0	0	16	0	19
Provincial leaders ineffective if opposed by departmental leaders	10	24	9	12	0	5
Departmental leaders effective despite provincial efforts at intervention	11	11	17	7	0	5
Did not know						
Not applicable, since did not perceive of provincial leaders' intervention	42	18	35	32	100	66
Number	100% (254)	100% (38)	100% (101)	100% (68)	100% (26)	100% (21)

ments' demands and the provincial leadership's demands could be fulfilled simultaneously. Under the system of proportional representation, however, the leadership's choice shrank to only one candidate of each type from each district. The reason was the party's electoral success: with each electoral victory the departmental leaders became more and more restive of this privilege of the provincial leaders. For the election of 1966 the provincial leadership was unable to enforce its own choices of candidates and had to content itself to exerting what pressure it could to obtain the best among the various factional candidates.

The Democratic Party's provincial leadership has always justified its privilege by arguing the need to insure the selection of technically qualified legislators. The leadership argued that the departmental leaders always selected their candidates upon the basis of purely political considerations: the performance of favors, the attraction of votes, the strength of factional support. Such candidates, furthermore, were chosen because of their ability to represent the narrow departmental interest. The provincial leadership argued that any legislative bloc needed members selected upon the basis of their capacity and preparation for the job who would reflect the broader, provincial interest. The leadership accepted the necessity of "political" candidates but argued that they should be complemented by some "technical" candidates.

The Radicals and Peronists, in contrast, stressed this reason less. While the Radical and Peronist parties' provincial leadership oftentimes spoke to the author of the similar need for technically qualified candidates, and while they often attempted to obtain such candidates, the provincial leadership of both groups had not developed the same traditional privilege, as part of the party process, as had the Democratic leadership. One explanation might be that neither controlled the provincial government, and, unlike the Conservatives, the provincial leadership of neither party grouping was as concerned or could not be as concerned about the selection of technically qualified candidates. Factionalism was the chief cause of intervention by the provincial leaders within the Radicals. The reason was twofold: the experience of the candidates of the Intransigent Radical Civic Union during and after the Frondizi Government, most of whom felt that candidacies were decided by personal conversations between the provincial leaders of each of the major factions; the factional fight within the Popular Radical Civic Union Party between the Popular Cause Faction and the Recuperation Faction. The Peronists cited factionalism as equally important as the need for capable candidates or the leadership's own peculiar choices as explanations for intervention. These last two explanations were equally, but secondarily, significant with the Radicals. Candidates from no party grouping considered provincial intervention to maintain internal factional equilibrium as significant. A significant number of Peronists and Christian Democrats cited other reasons as an explanation for intervention, which in these instances referred to the need for the provincial leadership to choose candidates because the departmental party was unorganized.

Among the factors preventing intervention by the provincial leadership, the Radicals and Conservatives emphasized more the role of previous consultation between the various levels of leadership within the provincial party than within the national party. The Radical and the Peronist candidates, also, emphasized the factor of no elective chance by the party as a more decisive barrier within the provincial party than within the national party. The Socialists almost entirely stressed party customs and party morality as the preventive of provincial intervention, while they merely included it along with party autonomy as a preventive of national intervention. For the Christian Democrats the party norms and morality were as equally important as party autonomy as a preventive of provincial intervention.

A comparison of Table V-3 and Table V-7 indicates a fundamental contrast between the methods of intervention used by the provincial party leadership and the methods of intervention used by the national party leadership. Generally, the style of intervention practiced by the provincial leadership is of an obstructive nature: to prevent, to stop, or to curtail a candidacy. Generally, the style practiced by the national leadership is of a supportive nature: to aid or to further a particular candidacy. This difference in styles between geographical levels of leadership is complemented by differences in styles between the provincial leadership of each party grouping. The Conservative leadership depended mostly upon the methods of persuasion and counseling: expressing the leaders' opinions or opposition concerning a candidacy. In contrast, the Radical leadership used some persuasion, but it relied more upon forceful methods: the veto, the location upon the ballot, and the counter-candidacy. As the Radicals, the Peronist leadership used some persuasion; but, in contrast to the other two party groupings, the Peronists' leadership actually named the candidates from the departments. Similarly, approximately twice as many Radicals and Peronists perceived non-intervention by the provincial leadership, the category of "not applicable", than did the Conservative candidates. These differences in styles of intervention assume significance when viewed along with perceptions about the effectiveness of this intervention.

All three party groupings, Conservatives, Radicals, and Peronists are alike in that approximately one fifth of the candidates of each grouping regarded provincial intervention as effective when it coincided with support by the departmental leadership. The differences between the three groupings concerned the distinct conclusions about the effectiveness of the provincial leaders' intervention when it encountered opposition from the departmental leadership. One fourth of the Conservatives viewed provincial intervention as effective despite opposition by the departmental leadership, while the same number viewed the departmental leadership as decisive in candidate selection, despite provincial intervention. In contrast, 17% of the Radical candidates felt that provincial intervention was effective, while approximately one half of that number felt that the departmental leadership was decisive. One tenth of the Peronist candidates viewed the provincial intervention as effective, while three times that number viewed the departmental leadership as decisive. Differences in each party grouping's elective position probably explain these statistical differences in the perception of the effective intervention by the provincial leadership as well as distinctiveness in the style of intervention practiced by the provincial leadership of each party grouping.

During the time period covered by this investigation, the Democratic Party controlled the provincial government. The provincial party leadership was thus forced to intervene in the selection of candidates to assure the nomination of: 1.) persons favorable to the governor's program; 2.) individuals at least creditably qualified for the position. One of the traditional rules of all Mendocine parties, with the exception of the Socialists, is the privilege of the party's gubernatorial nominee to insure the selection of at least some legislative candidates favorable to his point of view and program. Sometimes this privilege includes the right to veto any candidates, but this condition varies with both the situation and the party. The provincial party leadership was better able to enforce these demands by its manipulation of the "spoils of office": i.e., controls such as patronage, contracts, and favors. But just as the electoral success of the party increased the power of the provincial party leadership, it simultaneously increased the power of the departmental leadership vís-a-vís these provincial leaders. Mainly, the provincial leaders depended upon the departmental leaders for achieving and keeping a winning electoral coalition. Thus, the electoral success of the Democrats increased the ability of the provincial leadership to make and to enforce demands upon the departmental leadership (thus: one fourth of the party's candidates perceived provincial intervention as decisive despite opposition by departmental leaders). Meanwhile, it increased the power of the departmental leadership to resist authoritatively these demands (thus: one fourth of party's candidates perceived the departmental leadership as decisive despite provincial intervention). This relationship between the two levels of leadership explained the differences in the intervention style: the reliance upon persuasion and less dependence upon forceful methods.

While the Radicals did not control the provincial government, they did control the national government with its own "spoils of office." The Minister of Defense and the national director of the Y.P.F., the national oil company, were both provincial leaders of the Popular Cause Faction of the Mendocino Popular Radical Civic Union. The national Minister of the Post-office was a Mendocino closely associated with the party's provincial leaders of the Recuperation Faction. Postal patronage was dispensed upon the recommendation of the Recuperation leaders, while the patronage and favors of the Y.P.F. were dispensed by the leaders of the Popular Cause Faction. While the power of the provincial leaders (who had access to these national level controls) was increased, the power of the departmental leadership was not similarly increased. Actually, it was probably decreased, vís-a-vís these provincial leaders. Thus, the provincial leadership was able to make and to enforce its demands upon the departmental leaders (thus: 17% of the candidates perceived provincial intervention as decisive despite opposition by departmental leaders) while relying upon its own intervention style: methods of force. The departmental leaders were less able to oppose or to ignore successfully this intervention (thus: only nine percent of these party grouping's candidates perceived the departmental leadership as decisive despite provincial intervention).

The Peronists neither controlled the provincial government nor the national government, and had little hope of legitimately attaining either. (See Chapter I for the discussion of the Army Revolt of 1962 and its effect on the Peronists' chances to govern.) The characteristic of intervention by the provincial leadership was its nature: the selection of candidates when the departmental leadership itself could not or would not perform this function (the departments did not perform this function, or departmental opposition was absent, or departmental factions supported the provincial leaders). The provincial leadership was least likely to make and to enforce demands upon the departmental leadership (thus: only one tenth of the candidates perceived of provincial intervention as decisive despite opposition by departmental leaders). The Peronist leadership, likewise, depended upon the method of persuasion or actually selecting the candidates in the absence of departmental initiative. The situation of the Christian Democratic provincial leadership was similar to that of the Peronists, essentially for the same reason.

Mendocino politicians perceived of much greater articulation of the departmental party with the provincial party leadership, while they simultaneously perceived of much less articulation of the provincial party with the national party leadership. These Mendocino politicians would have asserted that the provincial party leadership was more effective in controlling the lower departmental levels of the party, and that this effectiveness increased in direct relationship to the electoral success of the party. The Tables show, furthermore, that not only were Mendocino political parties regarded as more centralized provincially, but also that Mendocino politicians regarded the provincial party leadership as actively attempting to intervene and to direct the party at the department-al levels. Only the Socialists were consistent in regarding their parties as decentralized provincially as well as nationally. These Mendocino politicians would have agreed with Michels that the provincial leader-ship willingly attempted centralization, but they would have disagreed with Michels that the provincial leadership was unable to achieve that centralization.[11]

The actual process of the selection of candidates was next examined to determine if the previous generalized feeling about centralization coin-cided with the reality of centralization within the Mendocino political parties. With the exception of the Socialist parties, almost all Mendo-cino political parties have traditionally had the following practice: the provincial party leadership has always formally approved the list of proposed pre-candidates either before the first formal nomination within the party or before the final nomination by a party primary or by the provincial convention, regardless of the particular candidacy. This practice poses the questions: 1.) To what extent was it formal approval only? 2.) To what extent did this formal approval coincide with or serve as a guise for practical intervention in the selection process? These same questions would also apply to the role of the party's national leader-ship, as well as to its provincial leadership.

Tables V-9 and V-10 indicate the degrees of formal approval of candidates by the provincial party leadership and by the national party leadership. Table V-9 shows that the national party leadership par-ticipated actively as well as merely formally to a significant degree only among the Peronists. The national party leadership tended to participate only formally within each of the other party groupings, while the provincial party leaders participated actively as well as merely formally in the nomination of one half or more of all candidacies in each of the elective party groupings. Among the non-elective parties none of the Socialist candidates experienced either active participation or merely formal approval by the provincial leaders in their selection.

A ready explanation for this condition of intervention by the national party leadership would be the tendency to continue national over-sight and management within the Peronist parties, as occurred during the Perón Government. Factionalism and the role of the party interventor to soften and to unify factional divisions really explain these differences between party groupings in the national leadership's formal approval of candidates. All Argentine political parties use the system of the national party interventor, who is appointed to this position by the national party leadership and who functions temporarily to manage or to oversee the provincial party organization. The national party interventor is generally considered to be used for four reasons: 1.) to maintain ideological purity

[11] *Ibid.*, pp. 195-201.

Table V-9

DEGREE OF FORMAL APPROVAL OF CANDIDATES BY THE NATIONAL PARTY LEADERSHIP WITHIN DIFFERENT PARTY GROUPINGS IN MENDOZA PROVINCE

Party grouping	Formal approval as well as participation in selection of candidates	Formal approval only; no participation in selection of candidates	Neither formal approval nor participation in selection of candidates	Did not know	Number
Conservative	0%	0%	100%	0%	100% (38)
Radical	4%	4%	85%	7%	100% (101)
Peronist	12%	12%	76%	0%	100% (68)
Socialist	0%	0%	100%	0%	100% (26)
Christian Democrat	0%	0%	91%	9%	100% (21)
All candidates	5%	5%	87%	3%	100% (254)

in a situation where the provincial party platform deviates from the national party platform by making the provincial one agree to the national one; 2.) to maintain the party's constitutional system in a situation where the provincial party leaders are disregarding or violating the party's Constitution or rules; 3.) to maintain provincial party unity in the nomination of candidates where party factionalism is so deep that an arbitrator must insure the selection of candidates most acceptable to all groups and factions; 4.) to bring the party rules and Constitution into accord with national laws and regulations concerning the political parties.

One cause of intervention within the Peronists certainly was the experience within the Blanco Party before the 1963 election. In this instance a coalition list of candidates was formed from the Blanco, the Justicialista parties, and various labor union movements. Within the Blanco Party the interventor served as assessor to assure the selection of ideologically committed candidates and to insure the fair representation of all groups. The national party interventor or the national party leadership actively participated in the selection of candidates. In no cases did this intervention function as an imposition, but rather as a necessary and arbitrary aid because of profound splits within the party. The Popular Union Party, furthermore, has always been intervened since its initiation in Mendoza Province, more to insure the continuation of the party, rather than its domination by the national leadership. The reason for the continuous intervention of the provincial party was to insure the existence of a provincial organization of the Popular Union Party in Mendoza. Since the Popular Union was the only national Peronist party with electoral recognition, it was hoped that by preserving a local party branch Perón would have a bargaining device with which to control the provincial independent Neo-Peronist leaders by the constant threat of presenting an opposing slate of candidates in any election by means of the Popular Union Party. The limited intervention within the Radicals occurred entirely within the Intransigent Radical Civic Union Party before the 1963 election when a final effort was made to maintain party unity before the decisive split between the present U.C.R.I. and the M.I.D. parties. The U.C.R.I. interventor served as a final arbitrator in determining the factional dispute.

Within the Mendocino parties the provincial party leadership, in contrast, very actively as well as merely formally participated in the selection of candidates among the elective party groupings. The Tables indicated that approval by the national party leadership was formal approval only. Approval by the provincial party leadership coincided with or served as a guise for practical and active intervention in the selection process within the elective party groupings. The extent of this active participation by the provincial leadership, furthermore, was statistically similar for all of the three elective party groupings. Only the

Table V-10

DEGREE OF FORMAL APPROVAL OF CANDIDATES BY THE PROVINCIAL PARTY LEADERSHIP WITHIN DIFFERENT
PARTY GROUPINGS IN MENDOZA PROVINCE

Party grouping	Formal approval as well as participation in selection of candidates	Formal approval only; no participation in selection of candidates	Neither formal approval nor participation in selection of candidates	Did not know	Number
Conservative	50%	34%	16%	0%	100% (38)
Radical	50%	44%	4%	2%	100% (101)
Peronist	53%	43%	4%	0%	100% (68)
Socialist	0%	0%	100%	0%	100% (26)
Christian Democrat	38%	43%	0%	19%	100% (21)
All candidates	45%	38%	16%	1%	100% (254)

Conservatives had a significant number of candidates selected without either formal or active participation by the provincial leadership. This unique condition of the Conservatives is probably explained by the extreme degree of independence of the departmental party leaders resulting from the provincial electoral success. Among the non-elective Socialists there was neither formal approval nor active participation in the selection of candidates by the provincial party leadership. Party norms and leadership's own morality caused this condition. The inability of the departmental leadership to select candidates explained the greater intensity of active participation by the provincial leaders within the non-elective Christian Democrats. Weak or unstructured party organizations in many departments caused the harried efforts by the provincial party leaders to seek and to obtain candidates to stand for election. Its recent appearance as a new political movement meant that the provincial leaders of the Christian Democrats had to contend with this very realistic problem in contrast to the long established Socialists.

Tables V-9 and V-10 showed the high ratio of active participation by the provincial party leadership in the selection of candidates and also showed that this high ratio was characteristic of all the party groupings with the exception of the Socialists. Both Tables demonstrated, furthermore, that the candidates' perception of intervention by the two levels of leadership corresponded to the reality of intervention by each of the levels of party leadership. Tables V-11 and V-12 examine the roles of the three levels of party leadership at each stage in the process to select candidates. Rather than examine the leaderships' role upon the usual basis of party grouping, since the overall general pattern was indicated by Tables V-9 and V-10, the following two Tables examine the leaderships' roles upon the basis of types of candidacies. The two types of candidacies were the district candidacies and the provincial candidacies. The term "district" candidates included candidates for provincial deputy and provincial senator. These candidates were nominated for an election within one of the three legislative districts into which Mendoza Province had been divided. The term "provincial" candidates included the candidates for provincial governor or national deputy. These candidates were nominated for an election upon a province-wide basis. This method of analysis was selected in order to give a more complete conceptualization of candidate selection in Mendoza Province as well as to test better the assertions originally posed at the beginning of this chapter.

Table V-11 demonstrates the roles of the departmental, the provincial, and the national parties' leadership at five different stages in the selection process. Table V-12 demonstrates the roles of these same leaderships at the screening stage of candidate selection. Alone, the national party leadership performed an insignificant role in the selection of candi-

Table V-11

SELECTION BY EACH LEVEL OF PARTY LEADERSHIP OF DISTRICT AND PROVINCIAL CANDIDATES AT CERTAIN NOMI-
NATING STAGES IN MENDOZA PROVINCE

Level of leadership	Stage of Pre-planning		Stage of Instigation		Stage of Presentation		Stage of Binding nomination		Stage of Ballot Location	
	Dist.	Prov.	Dist.	Prov.	Dist.	Prov.	Dist.	Prov.	Dist.	Prov.
Departmental leadership only	55%	2%	46%	15%	61%	10%	40%	4%	18%	7%
Departmental and provincial leadership	5	11	7	5	7	20	6	8	19	2
Provincial leadership only	25	64	23	61	16	61	31	65	41	18
Provincial/departmental as well as national leadership	2	10	1	0	1	0	0	0	12	60
National leadership only	1	0	3	5	1	0	1	5	1	2
Did not know or not-leadership elements	12	13	20	14	14	9	22	18	9	11
	100%	100%	100%	100%	100%	100%	100%	100%	100%	100%
	(210)	(44)	(210)	(44)	(210)	(44)	(210)	(44)	(210)	(44)

Table V-12

PARTICIPATION BY EACH LEVEL OF PARTY LEADERSHIP AT THE SCREEN-
ING STAGE OF DISTRICT AND PROVINCIAL CANDIDATES IN MENDOZA
PROVINCE

Level of leadership	Support of candidacy		Opposition to candidacy	
	Dist.	Prov.	Dist.	Prov.
Departmental leadership	71%	69%	30%	25%
Provincial leadership	65	89	24	39
National leadership	12	16	0	2
	(Figures are overlapping and do not total 100%)			
	(210)	(44)	(210)	(44)

Note: The low figures regarding opposition to a candidacy were caused by the unwillingness of the respondents to expose information unfavorable to their candidacy.

dates. Their statistical insignificance, furthermore, was the same at
any and all stages of the nomination process. Similarly, this statistical
insignificance applied to the selection of district level candidacies as well
as to provincial level candidacies. The only significant role of the national party leadership occurred at the stages of pre-planning, screening,
and location of the provincial candidates. The significance, however, of
the national leaders was only in conjunction with other provincial elements of the leadership. The condition that the national leadership was
never significant by itself merely indicated again the supportive nature
of national activity: the expression of opinion, or activity in aid of a
certain candidacy. The role of the national leader was, essentially, in
participation with or at the toleration of the provincial elements of the
leadership. The national leaders had a high degree of interest in the
ballot location of the provincial level candidacies, because this type of
candidacy included the national legislators who would occupy national
positions and thus help to determine the national party's image.

The Tables, in contrast, show a different and generally consistent
pattern in the roles discharged by each level of the provincial parties'
leadership elements in the selection of each type of candidacy. The
activity of the departmental level leadership was toward the management
and oversight of the nomination of district level candidacies. Clearly
the tendency was for the departmental leaders to dominate the selection
of district candidates. The activity of the provincial level leadership was
toward the management and oversight of the nomination of provincial
candidates. Clearly the tendency was for the provincial leaders to
dominate the selection of provincial level candidacies. There was a
definite correlation between the type of candidacy and the role of each
level of the provincial party leadership in the selection of candidates.
The provincial leaders were more decisive, either alone or in conjunction
with other levels of leadership, in the selection of the district level

candidacies, than the departmental leaders were in the selection of provincial level candidacies, either alone or in conjunction with other levels of leadership. This situation suggested that the provincial leaders tended more to encroach upon the nomination of candidacies which ideally belonged to the departmental level of leadership. While there was encroachment, there was no displacement of the departmental leadership by the provincial leadership.

The role of both the departmental and provincial leadership significantly increased at the screening stage, regardless of the type of candidacy. The role of the provincial leadership significantly increased at the stage of the location upon the ballot, while the role of the departmental leadership significantly decreased. The explanation would be that, generally, the determination of the ballot position of all candidates has been considered a decision of the provincial leadership essentially. The surprising situation is that the figure of ballot location by the departmental leadership is so high; the previous experience with the Mendocino Radicals, Conservatives, and Peronists, would have suggested that the figure should have been much lower or nil. Increasingly, the departmental leadership has begun assuming more and more decisive participation in this stage. Traditionally, the decision as to the ballot position of all candidates has been the prerogative exclusively of the provincial Central Committee of the Democratic Party. This prerogative was never successfully challenged until the election of 1965 when the departmental leaders of the Third Electoral District forced the Central Committee to put the departmental choices in the first four places. Furthermore, the departmental leaders forced the provincial Central Committee to eliminate one provincial legislator whom the Committee had re-nominated and put in an elective position upon the ballot. Again, in the 1966 election the departmental leaders of the First and Third Districts forced the Central Committee to re-arrange its ordering of candidates. Electoral success of the party is the chief explanation for this new revolt of the departmental leadership. Within Mendocino parties there has been a change from exclusive control of this prerogative by the provincial party leadership to its sharing with other leadership elements. The intensity of the provincial level leadership at this particular stage, however, suggested that ballot location was still the chief method to oppose successfully unwanted candidacies and to insure successfully desired candidacies. While the provincial leadership could not veto or replace an unwanted candidacy indiscriminately, it could at least prevent their election by means of manipulation of the ballot position.

From the stage of pre-planning to the stage of ballot location the provincial party leadership dominated the management and control of the selection of the national legislative-gubernatorial candidates. Although there was significant participation by the departmental leadership, this participation tended to be more of a supportive nature. The greatest activity of the departmental leadership occurred during the screening stage, but with no significant role at the stages of the binding nomination or the location upon the ballot. All of which indicated that its role was more to express approval or disapproval of proposed candidacies. The provincial leadership may have dominated the selection process, but the departmental leadership participated in a cooperative-consultative role. The departmental leadership operated as a restraint: while it did not itself choose the national legislative-gubernatorial candidates, the departmental leadership did restrain the provincial leadership from the selection of candidates obviously unwanted or profoundly opposed by the departmental leaders. In their selection of this type of candidates the provincial leadership had to keep the departmental leadership's attitudes in mind and could not act entirely as a free agent.

The stages of the pre-planning, the instigation, and the presentation of the provincial legislative candidates was clearly dominated by the departmental leadership. The greatest activity of the provincial leadership occurred at the screening stage, where the provincial leadership expressed its approval or disapproval. The provincial leadership, furthermore, participated in a much more significantly effective manner at the stage of the binding nomination and determined to a greater extent the ballot position. The statistics suggested that while the departmental leadership could initiate its own candidacies, the provincial leadership could more successfully enforce its own expectations and demands upon the departmental leadership in the selection of departmental (provincial legislative) candidates, then the departmental party leadership could exert upon the provincial leadership in the selection of the provincial (national legislative-gubernatorial) candidates.

CHAPTER VI

AN EVALUATION OF CANDIDATE RECRUITMENT
IN MENDOZA PROVINCE

This investigation demonstrated that certain commonly made assertions are not, upon the basis of each party grouping's certification
of its candidates, validly accurate identifications of that political party
grouping with certain socio-economic groups in Mendocino society.
The reasons were twofold. One reason was the condition that the
candidates of all party groupings fundamentally tended to share certain
common socio-economic characteristics. Fundamentally, for example,
the candidates of any party grouping tended to be members of the middle
classes and descendents of immigrant stock with foreign parentage. The
candidates of all party groupings, then, tended toward a certain fundamental similarity in socio-economic background. This investigation, however, did demonstrate the possible usefulness of these assertions as
showing the existence of certain biases or tendencies of each political
grouping to represent certain socio-economic groups within Mendocino
society. Yet, while these certain biases or tendencies did characterize
each political movement in the selection of its candidates, still each
political grouping selected candidates having heterogeneous and sometimes, contradictory, socio-economic qualities. Although this characteristic is a second reason against the validity of these commonly made
assertions, it is a decisively significant and important characteristic of
each political movement, in the opinion of the author.

Each political party grouping, in differing degrees of extensiveness
and completeness, represented a cross-section of Mendocino society
among its candidates. The best example, perhaps, was Radicalism, a
political movement which nominated as its candidates elements from
every type or kind within the socio-economic schema of society. This
characteristic of Radicalism as a representative of diverse socio-economic
elements within the society has been the most frequent criticism made
against it as a political movement.[1] The criticism made against Radicalism has been that it never resolved the need to define its ideology and
its politico-governmental program and the impossibility to make such
a definition of policy or program because it would splinter the diverse
membership elements which composed Radicalism and caused its rupture
as a unified political movement. An example of such a rupture was the
split between the Popular Radical Civic Union and the Intransigent

[1] See Silvio Frondizi, *Doce años de política argentina*, p. 25.

Radical Civic Union in 1958. Yet, the same criticism, or assessment, could have been made about any of the Mendocino political movements examined in this investigation.

An evaluation of the representative character of the Mendocino political party groupings would be determined by these simultaneously contradictory tendencies of all party grouping's candidates: the tendency that any grouping's candidates fundamentally shared certain common socio-economic characteristics; and the counter-tendency that any grouping's candidates contained heterogeneous and sometimes, contradictory, socio-economic qualities. These two tendencies of Mendocino party groupings suggest that these party groupings failed to fulfill ideally either of two general theories of representation. One theory of representation argues that the legislature needs to be a miniature of the larger society. The legislature needs to be more nearly similar to the total representation of the community, by means of each legislator resembling closely the community he represents. Thus, the under-representation of various socio-economic groups of the society within the legislature is a sign toward the dangerous condition of elitism.[2] Essentially, all grouping's candidacies were members of the middle-class, despite the continuing socio-economic biases or tendencies of each. The middle-class provided the core of each grouping's candidacies, regardless of whether this core was biased toward the lower middle class stratum or toward the upper middle class stratum. In effect, each political movement seemed to reflect the new positive political role of the middle classes in Latin American society.[3] The fact that the party groupings basically selected candidates tending to share a similar socio-economic background suggests the impossibility of fulfilling this theory of representation. Such a situation, however, also suggests the need for another investigation to correlate the socio-economic characteristics of the candidates with the socio-economic characteristics of the particular constituencies which they represent. This investigation would be a means to test empirically if, in fact, the party groupings do or do not fulfill this theory of representation in their selection of candidates. The opposite theory of representation argues that the community is best served by legislators who form a superior elite to the community's inhabitants, and that the legislature is not to be a microcosm of the whole society. While the candidates' tendency toward a common background would have impelled them toward this condition of elitism, their counter-tendency toward diversity prevented the candidates from ideally fulfilling this elite condition.

This diversity among the candidates' background suggests another evaluation of Mendocino party groupings. The candidates do form an elite from the strictly functional point of view, in the sense that: they are

[2] See James David Barber, *The Lawmakers*, pp. 250-251.
[3] J. J. Johnson, *Political Change in Latin America*, pp. 192-194.

the persons who discharge the elective role of party candidates; or, if elected, they will discharge the government positions of the provincial society. In the mere functional sense Mendocino party groupings do provide a plurality of individuals who can govern. The candidates' diversity in background, however, makes it impossible to speak of them as a leadership elite. Such a leadership elite would consist of individuals who conduct the society's affairs in concert in order to obtain certain common goals, either expressly or tacitly agreed upon among themselves. Similar norms and values would guide the members of this leadership elite in its conduct and management of society's affairs. This investigation demonstrated the dissimilar extractions in the social background between the candidates of the party groupings. This dissimilarity, in turn, caused differences in socialization among the candidates. During their formative period the candidates did not experience a similar schooling and formation. The candidates did not share common experiences or references, nor were they presently united as a nucleus by the same entity, such as a political party or a private club or some similar type of institution. Their diversity meant that the candidates did not and could not communicate by means of a common dialogue. During their formative period the candidates did not have any face to face contact or experience with one another from which to develop a common dialogue. Nor had they subsequently developed such contacts or had such experiences. This characteristic of the Mendocino political party groupings' candidates is similar to the characteristic of Argentina's governing groups. Argentina, also, has not had a leadership elite since the 1920's.[4] During the 1880's and the 1890's Argentina was governed by such a leadership elite, consisting of a small self-restricted group who exercised the leadership of the society. This traditional Oligarchy was characterized by members coming from the same families, experiencing the same educational establishments and formation, and participating in the same social clubs. Although this traditional Oligarchy had no explicit political program, it did develop and implement such a program implicitly by means of common association, actions, and reactions. This situation suggests the need for another research investigation of Mendocino legislators and legislative candidates similar to that made of Argentine legislators by Cantón. A comparison should be made of the socio-economic characteristics of candidates chosen by the different party groupings in the earlier period(s) to determine if there has been a significant change in the social class basis of candidate selection in Mendoza Province.

This investigation has demonstrated the impossibility of applying Michels' assertions about the "iron law of oligarchy" impartially to all Mendocino political parties. Basically Michels wanted to demonstrate that the condition of oligarchy inevitably developed in the newer Socialist mass parties just as it had already developed in the older traditional

[4] José Luis de Imaz, *Los que mandan*, pp. 239-240.

Conservative parties. Michels, actually, considered the Socialist parties the worst offenders, since they so publicly proclaimed their democratic organization and functioning, and since this type of party had originated in opposition to the prevailing condition of oligarchy within political parties.[5] This investigation showed that Michels' conclusions about the "iron law of oligarchy" were inapplicable to the Mendocino Socialist parties, but were applicable to the other political movements with varying degrees of intensity. Within the Socialist parties the mass membership managed the selection process, whereas within the other political groupings the mass membership was insignificant or was significant only at a certain few stages in the selection process. Rather than being the worst offenders, as Michels would have predicted, the Socialist parties were actually the best achievers. A distinct condition, however, applied to the other political parties in Mendoza. Fundamentally, but not entirely, the other parties were governed by an oligarchical party leadership. Fundamentally, but not entirely, the party leadership effectively managed and controlled the selection process. This management and control by the leadership was incomplete at three stages of the selection process: enlistment, screening, and binding nomination. At these three stages of selection the not-leadership elements did participate in the selection of candidates: to a significant degree within the Popular Radical Civic Union Party and to lesser degrees of intensity within various other parties. Yet, while it is thus impossible to classify the other parties as examples of pure oligarchies, fundamentally and practically any assertions about their oligarchical nature would apply to these other parties. In each of these provincial political parties an oligarchical party leadership effectively selected the legislative and gubernatorial candidates. This investigation limited itself by examining only one aspect of the Mendocino political parties: the process of candidate recruitment. Other necessary investigations would have to examine the political and party careers of these same candidates, as well as other aspects of the Mendocino political party process, in order to determine more fully the reality of oligarchy in Mendocino political parties.

Michels listed three types of causes for the development of oligarchy: technical, psychological, and the nature of the political struggle.[6] The fundamental technical causes were two: 1.) the physical impossibility of the membership making decisions and its consequent necessity to assign this function to delegates; 2.) the indespensibility of the leadership because of its vast experience, which meant that only it could solve the difficult and intricate questions and problems inevitably facing the political party. Michels was pessimistic about the uses of the referendum, while wholly rejecting anarchism and syndicalism, as solutions (prophylactics)

[5] Robert Michels, *Political Parties*, p. 11; R. T. McKenzie, *British Political Parties*, pp. 15-16, 644.
[6] Michels, *Political Parties*, p. viii.

for these technical causes of oligarchy.[7] The Socialist experience, however, with the mail ballot as the method for selecting candidates demonstrated that the membership could decide directly itself and need not award its decision-making function to delegates. The fundamental psychological causes for oligarchy were three: 1.) the membership's increasing veneration of the leadership and its consequently complete dependence upon the leadership for guidance; 2.) the general indifference and consequent non-participation of the membership in party affairs; 3.) the moral change in the leadership making it eventually substitute its own personal interests for the entire party's interests.[8] Michels was pessimistic about the possibility of an active and interested public opinion or of economic and social renunciation by the party leadership as solutions for these psychological causes.[9] The indifference of the average citizen to political activity and political party affairs has been a common criticism by students of Argentina.[10] The Socialist system for the selection of candidates enforces the membership's active participation in the selection process while it enables the membership's independence of the leadership. Yet, the success of the Socialist system has depended basically upon the party leaders' own moral restraints. The Socialist leaders have tended to remain faithful to Justo's own concept of the Socialist movement's main purpose as that of training or preparing the workers for political participation rather than that of merely winning elections.[11] The third type of causes, never adequately examined nor extensively developed by Michels, was the nature of the political struggle. One of the factors influencing the activity and functioning of the Mendocino Socialist parties (and of the Argentine Socialist movement) was that: either it was never an electoral majority party; or it never enjoyed any serious chance of legitimately gaining control and management of the provincial (and of the national) government. Between 1912 and 1930 the Socialist Party functioned under the unlikelihood that it would be allowed to gain and to keep control of either the national government or any provincial government by legitimate means. Its situation, then, was comparable to the same situation regarding the present-day Peronist Movement. Perhaps the internal functioning of the party would have changed had it enjoyed any serious chance of becoming an electoral majority or had it effectively controlled the government for a long period of time.

This investigation, however, did demonstrate the possibility of an-

[7] *Ibid.*, pp. 25-27, 80-89, 335-336, 355, 360.

[8] *Ibid.*, pp. 49-52, 60-64, 205.

[9] *Ibid.*, pp. 406-407, 443-444.

[10] L. S. Rowe, *The Federal System of the Argentine Republic*, p. 81; Agustín P. Rivero Astengo, *Juárez Celman: 1844-1909*, pp. 220-223; J. N. Matienzo, *El gobierno representativo*, p. 339.

[11] Cúneo, *Juan B. Justo y las luchas sociales en la Argentina*, p. 140.

other type of solution as a corrective or preventive of oligarchy. The experience of the Mendocino Popular Radical Civic Union demonstrated the possibility of intra-party factionalism as a corrective of the oligarchical condition. Although Michels did examine the situation of intra-party factionalism, he specifically rejected it is a corrective or preventive of oligarchy.[12] Yet, the experience of the U.C.R.P. did show that conflict between two or more internal party factions over the selection of candidates did increase the membership's activity and effective participation in the decision-making process. This same factor and its similar effects functioned in isolated instances within the Conservative and the Peronist party groupings. This factionalism functioned as a sort of checking and balancing system within the party's leadership and consequently lessened the condition of oligarchy. Michels could not foresee the possibility of an internal checking and balancing system between the party membership and the leadership as a preventive of oligarchy. He failed to foresee, however, the possibility of such a check and balance system between factions of the party leadership as a preventive of oligarchy.

Michels defined his democracy-oligarchy continuum as follows: the greater condition of democracy is achieved as the number of the participants in the decision-making process increases to 100% of the membership, with the condition of pure democracy being the condition of complete participation; the greater condition of oligarchy is achieved as the participants in power decreases to only 1% of the membership, with the condition of pure oligarchy being the condition of one man rule. Using this loose operational definition of democracy-oligarchy, the Mendocino political parties would be located upon the democracy-oligarchy continuum in somewhat the following manner:

SOCIALISTS	U.C.R.P.		DEMOCRATS	M.P.M. CHRISTIAN DEMOCRATS	ALL OTHER PARTIES		POPULAR UNION
//		//					//

100%   51%// 49%   1%
Pure Democracy   Pure Oligarchy
(total participation   (one-man
of the membership)   decisions)

[12] Michels, *Political Parties,* pp. 164-168.

Michels was aware of the factor of federalism as affecting the location but not the existence of oligarchy. Michels clearly distinguished between the condition of party oligarchy and the condition of party centralization-decentralization, although sometimes the two distinct conditions have become confused.[18] In a political party having two geographical levels of leadership Michels foresaw the inevitable conflict of each level of leadership, one with another. The lower level of leadership constantly sought freedom (equilibrium) from control or direction by the higher level of the leadership, but the general tendency always was toward the condition of centralization. Michel's awareness of this factor of centralization resulted from his examination of the Social Democratic Party of Germany, the party which he mainly used as the empirical evidence from which to develop his assertions. At that time the Social Democratic Party of Germany was a national party with no possibility of control or of participation in the state (provincial) governments. Also, the state (provincial) party organizations lacked the means to become independent from the national leadership's influences because of the basic nature of the party as a national party only. The condition of centralization, thus, appeared to be a more natural condition of the party and consequently of any political party. From his examination of the German Socialist experience Michels even presumed that the North American political parties likewise would be characterized by this condition of centralization.[14]

The parties examined by this study, however, were either individually separate provincial organizations or were independent provincial organizations operating as part of a national party. The distinctive characteristic of these parties was that they were decentralized nationally. Although intervention by the national party leaders in the selection process occurred, this intervention was in an auxiliary sense rather than in a managerial, decisive sense. The activity of the national leadership was either only to aid their favorite provincial candidates or to act as arbitrators between unalterable provincial party factions. The national party leadership did not impose any candidates. Also, this investigation did demonstrate that the Radicals' and the Socialists' assertions, that their parties were federal in structure and in practice, were valid within the national party organizations. This investitigation did not examine the relationship between the selection of candidates and those historico-institutional factors which would have encouraged nationally governmental centralization or those historico-institutional factors which would have discouraged such nationally governmental centralization. This investigation did demonstrate, however, that the commonly made assertions by students of the Argentine that the political

[18] An example of this confusion is Samuel J. Eldersveld, *Political Parties: a behavioral analysis.*

[14] Michels, *Political Parties*, p. 179.

parties are inevitably centralized nationally were not validated by the Mendocino experience. Mendocino political parties would have tended to support those assertions which classify Argintina as having an operating federal system, which includes nationally decentralized political parties.

But the Mendocino political parties could not be classified as purely decentralized political parties provincially, nor could they be classified as purely centralized political parties provincially. In no party grouping was there any evidence of complete localism nor was there any evidence of complete central management and control by the provincial leadership. Mendocino party groupings, actually, occupied an in-between position between the two ideal conditions. They would have been located somewhere upon the continuum between the ideal condition of provincial centralization and departmental decentralization. Each grouping's location upon this continuum and each group's tendency/counter-tendency toward centralization or decentralization would have been determined by certain conditions and situations at the moment. The evidence demonstrated that the condition of provincial electoral success, as with the Democrats, intensified both the tendency toward centralization and the counter-tendency toward decentralization. National electoral success, as with the Popular Radical Civic Union, without a corresponding provincial electoral success intensified the tendency toward centralization and probably abated the counter-tendency toward decentralization. The absence of both national and provincial electoral success combined with the presence as an electoral majority, as with the Peronists, intensified the counter-tendency toward decentralization while it increased the activity and role of the provincial leadership—but in a different sense than that implied by the term "centralization."

Michels listed eight types of internal party disputes which caused party factionalism.[15] The most common types were disputes over party ideology and party policy, or disputes between leaders because of personality clashes. Tables VI-1 and VI-2 suggest the importance of these types of disputes within the Mendocino political party groupings. As part of their interview all candidates were requested to rank four types of internal party disputes according to their order of importance within the provincial party, as well as between the provincial party leadership and the national party leadership.

Both Tables demonstrate the importance of the selection process in three party groupings : the Conservatives, the Radicals, and the Peronists. Within the Radical and the Peronist provincial parties disputes over the nomination of candidates had more importance than other types of disputes. In contrast, ideological disputes (both within the provincial party and between the provincial and national leaderships) were decisive,

[15] *Ibid.*, pp. 167-168.

Table VI-1

TYPE OF DISPUTE WITHIN THE PROVINCIAL PARTY WHICH WAS RANKED IN FIRST PLACE BY CANDIDATES OF DIFFERENT PARTY GROUPINGS IN MENDOZA PROVINCE

Type of dispute	Total	Conservative	Radical	Peronist	Socialist	Christian Democrat
Ideology and party policy	45%	46%	35%	34%	91%	72%
Selection of candidates	33	31	37	46	4	14
Positions of party power	8	3	12	5	0	14
Personal disputes between the leaders	14	20	16	15	5	0
Number	100% (232)	100% (35)	100% (92)	100% (67)	100% (23)	100% (21)

Note: This Table is based upon 232 responses, since 22 candidates did not or could not make this ranking.

Table VI-2

TYPE OF DISPUTE BETWEEN PROVINCIAL PARTY LEADERSHIP AND NATIONAL PARTY LEADERSHIP WHICH WAS RANKED IN FIRST PLACE BY CANDIDATES OF DIFFERENT PARTY GROUPINGS IN MENDOZA PROVINCE

Type of dispute	Total	Conservative	Radical	Peronist	Socialist	Christian Democrat
Ideology and party policy	59%	69%	46%	56%	95%	79%
Selection of candidates	18	12	28	11	0	6
Positions of party power	10	6	10	18	0	5
Personal disputes between the leaders	13	13	16	15	5	10
Number	100% (182)	100% (16)	100% (83)	100% (45)	100% (19)	100% (19)

Note: This Table was based upon 182 responses, since 72 candidates did not or could not make this ranking.

while such nomination disputes were insignificant in the Socialist and the Christian Democratic party groupings. A difference between the major ideological groups in elective possibilities would have explained this difference in the responses of the candidates. Both the Christian Democrats and the Socialists consisted of minor parties without any elective possibilities: the Christian Democrats had never elected a candidate for any office in Mendoza Province; the Socialists had become electorally insignificant, although still managing to elect a few municipal councilmen under the system of proportional representation. The Tables suggested that the candidates of these minor party movements conceived of their parties as performing essentially the similar role performed by the minor parties in the United States. In both regions the minor parties were ideologically, rather than electorally, oriented. The minor parties served the function of formulating new policies and programs and of calling attention to necessary reforms in the society.[16] The other three party groupings contained the political parties having elective possibilities: the Democrats, the Popular Radical Civic Union, the Intransigent Radical Civic Union, the Popular Movement of Mendoza, the Blanco, and the Tres Banderas parties. These parties were electorally, rather than ideologically, oriented and thus disputes centered around candidates' nomination. Factors of centralization/decentralization within the provincial party explained the greater importance of the nomination of candidates within the provincial party. Their condition as nationally decentralized parties explained the lesser importance of these types of disputes between the provincial and the national party leaderships within all party groupings.

[16] See William B. Hesseltine, *The Rise and Fall of Third Parties*, pp. 9-10.

APPENDIX: NOTES ON METHODOLOGY

The author lived for two and one half years in the Province of Mendoza. In the first stage of his investigation the author devoted the first year familiarizing himself with the Argentine and the Mendocino cultures and to learning the language, generally by two methods: auditing courses at the School of Political Science and the Faculty of Philosophy of the University of Cuyo and extensive self-directed reading. The purpose of these activities was to give the author a general knowledge as well as to allow him to perform basic background research for this book. The fundamental background research on Mendocino political development and contemporary political reality was achieved by reading all issues of the major provincial newspaper, *Los Andes,* 1930 until 1966 and compiling an extensive series of notes about specific political situations. The author needed about one year in which to learn the language well enough so that he could speak confidently with any person of whatever educational background or accent. The period of time was required despite the fact that the author had studied Spanish in high school and was married to a Mendocino university professor who spoke to him only in Spanish. When the author first began his interviews, he lost about 25% to 33% of the conversation in "wastage." After a few months his conversational loss varied from 5% to a 10% maximum. The chief problem was that of names, perhaps the most vital element in indicating what exactly occurred in the selection process. His Anglo-Saxon background meant that the author's ears were not attuned to the meatier Italo-Spanish names; and originally much confusion resulted, because while the author understood the events correctly, he was unable to associate the happenings with the correct actors.

Then this author felt prepared and confident enough to begin the second stage of his investigation; the actual survey research. The author prepared a questionnaire with two purposes in mind. One purpose was to include those questions which would allow him most accurately and most adequately to probe the recruitment of candidates within the realities of the Mendocino political culture. The other purpose was to achieve most effectively the original goals of this investigation as well as certain new goals formulated after his location in Mendoza Province for one year. After writing his questionnaire the author tested it by interviewing twenty-five candidates. The first fifteen respondents were former political party activists or legislators, all of whom were no longer active politically and had been candidates long before the period of 1962-1965. During those test interviews the author was not concerned with the respondents' accuracy or ability to recall facts. Rather the author was concerned with two situations: gauging the respondent's reaction to the interview and his willingness to answer the questions of the interview; and gauging the applicability of the questionnaire to the Mendocino political party reality. After these test interviews the author discussed the respondent's reaction to the questionnaire and in several instances obtained criticisms and suggestions about specific questions. These comments helped in eliminating ambiguities in the phrasing of the questionnaire and in clarifying the author's own thinking about the purposes of some questions. The author next interviewed ten legislative-gubernatorial candidates from the elections of 1962 and 1963. The purpose of these interviews was to create the actual interview situation; and the author was concerned, not only with gauging the respondent's reactions and responsiveness, but also in developing his ability to manage the interview situation and in determining the applicability of the interview to contemporary political party process.

This author then began interviewing with his questionnaire partially revised after this period of pre-testing. The interview was arranged to consist of two parts: the standard questionnaire, whose answers were recorded by the author during the interview and which gathered data about the candidate's social background, nomination, and opinions; a subsequent depth-interview which ranged in length and topics according to the particular circumstances. The depth-interview probed more deeply into the candidate's knowledge of his own nomination as well as to cross-check information about the nomination of other candidates within his own political party. No notes were taken during this depth interview; afterward the information was written on file cards when the author was alone. Simultaneously, the author noted on a separate card his own impressions about the respondent's reactions to the interview, the respondent's openness and eagerness to help, and the respondent's apparent reliability.

The actual interviewing began in September of 1965 and was concluded in October of 1966. During this year the author was able to complete 254 interviews out of approximately 400 scheduled interviews. This figure of only a 63% response does not accurately reflect the author's success in interviewing. From September of 1965 until February of 1966 the author was able to conduct only 110 interviews out of approximately 250 scheduled interviews. These successful interviews were conducted largely with candidates from all parties who were friends of the author's wife (a native of Mendoza Province) or of his wife's family or with candidates from the Intransigent Radical Civic Union, the Movement for Integration and Development, and the Christian Democrats. The explanation for access to family friends is obvious. The reason for access to candidates from these three specific parties was (in the opinion of the author) due to the fact that none of these parties enjoyed any chance of electoral success and that their candidates were either recently "retired" or "just starting" political activists who did not regard the author's investigation as a threat either to their own political career or to their political party. The lack of any sponsorship of the author explains the paucity of interviews over this five month period and the condition that 140 scheduled interviews were never carried out. Initially, for the first year and one-half the author did not enjoy any sponsorship.

For a long time the author had to work alone, unannounced, and unintroduced. Only in April, 1966, did the author secure the sponsorship of a university professor who was excited by the proposed study and wished to see it completed. With the enthusiastic sponsorship of his investigation by the Director of the Institute of Sociology of the University of Cuyo the author was able to conduct 144 interviews with candidates of all parties in the four month period from June to October of 1966. These 144 completed interviews were carried out from a total of 150 attempted interviews. Of these six incomplete interviews, two were caused by the refusal to be interviewed, while four were scheduled but had to be given up because of genuine excuses by either the author or the candidates. The author did not schedule any interviews from March until the middle of June of 1966 because of the concern of the political party leaders with a provincial election in April of 1966.

Survey research by North American social scientists is usually based upon the use of the "random sample" survey. This author intentionally did not use the random sample; rather he purposely conducted a biased survey and attempted to get interviews with the candidates located in the first six positions of the ballot. Of these 254 interviews 133 (52%) were with candidates occupying the first three ballot positions, 70 (28%) were with candidates occupying the second three ballot positions, and 51 (20%) were with candidates occupying the last six ballot positions. The random sample was rejected because, first, the newness of this type of study made the author dependent upon interviews from whomever he could obtain them. Also, the author felt that only the significant party leaders and political actors occupied the first six positions. With very few exceptions the remaining positions were filled by party hacks. The author found from experience that these persons demanded a much more difficult, exasperating, and time consuming interview; too, the information obtained was skimpy and hearsay. Generally only the major party leaders could give an accurate picture of the nomination process. While the random sample might have given a fuller resume of the social characteristics, it would have given a more inaccurate picture of the nomination process. The author felt that the biased sample eliminated such unaccurate and misleading information. In summary, the biased survey gave a better indication of the factors really decisive in each party's nomination of its candidates.

Two determinants of the success of any survey research are the respondents' accessibility and the respondents' responsiveness. The initial difficulty of accessibility to the political actors disappeared after the investigator achieved sponsorship by the director of the Institute of Sociology. After obtaining his sponsorship the investigator not only found that he had access to all political actors (with only two exceptions) but that he also had access to the major provincial party leaders. In a minority of instances, this investigator pleasantly discovered that his position was reversed; instead of having to seek out the respondents and to assume the entire initiative in getting an interview, approximately one dozen of the proposed respondents sought out the investigator and initiated the interview themselves.

One of the common opinions in Argentine society, and especially among the academic community in Mendoza, is that the politicians are habitual liars, somewhat immoral, and entirely amoral. This author has just the opposite opinion: he felt that the politicians whom he interviewed were basically honest. Among all 254 interviews, the investigator knew of only three candidates who deliberately falsified information. As Sorauf, this author found that the politicians were honest and direct in answering questions,[1] but such honesty should not be confused with openness. The politicians gave that information which presented their actions or their reputations most favorably. Any contrary information was simply suppressed unless it was brought into the conversation by the author, in which case it was answered fully. The politicians never volunteered the information; they were careful always to let the author exercise the initiative.

Except for one question, all respondents answered all questions of the questionnaire, but these answers varied from the briefest information necessary to long rambling statements packed with information and hearsay about the candidate himself as well as about other candidates. This investigator generally felt that the "don't know" responses actually represented the respondents' lack of knowledge and were not stratagems for withholding information. It was, however, during the subsequent depth interview that the author encountered resistance and outright refusal to answer questions. It is interesting to note that if major party leaders or members of the upper class did not want to answer a question, they bluntly refused to respond. Middle class persons tried to be evasive, while lower class persons simply stated the information. The greatest difficulty was to get the respondents to give the names of the actors in a given situation. Oftentimes the actors were designated by letters or by the impersonal pronoun; and no amount of assurance by the author about the anonymity of the interviews changed this unwillingness. The best sources of information concerning specific names and events about any nomination were the members of the lower class or the

[1] See Frank J. Sorauf, *Party and Representation*, p. 158.

upper class; middle class candidates, and especially lower middle class candidates, were reticent. The higher position a candidate occupied within the party hierarchy, the more openly and willingly he answered with specific information. With few exceptions the major party leaders willingly answered all questions in substantial detail, when asked; they were careful never to volunteer the information themselves. The author never felt any need to be restrained in the questions that he asked. He felt that most of the decisive political actors were quite willing to give any information requested and to discuss any opinions or hearsay, especially if it concerned themselves.

Generally the most difficult and time-consuming part of the questionnaire was the questions about the candidate's own social characteristics, probably because of the old Spanish tradition of keeping one's private life secret.[2] Oftentimes, the author was aware that the respondent felt as if he had been "stripped naked" after answering the first sixteen questions. The fact, furthermore, that several candidates were illegitimate children and most candidates were descendents of recent immigrant families meant that many candidates were probably embarrassed by their lack of certain commonly assumed knowledge about themselves or their paternal families. The easiest portion of the study concerned the questions about the nomination process. That is not to say that the respondents talked openly and willingly, but that they had less difficulty in answering this type of question.

A major frustration concerned the interview itself. The author felt that for every hour of interview he had to spend ten hours in the simple mechanics of finding the person, meeting the person and introducing himself, arranging the interview, and then returning for a successful interview. Initially the author suffered from the problem of broken appointments—some reasonably, but most intentionally unkept. This problem disappeared after the author achieved sponsorship.

Originally the author tried to conduct the entire interview impromptu, but he very soon developed the habit of leaving a copy of the printed questionnaire with the prospective respondent. The reasons were several: 1) it allowed the respondent to decide definitely if he wanted to complete the interview, or, hopefully, to forewarn the author if the interview was to be cancelled; 2) it allowed some of the candidates to prepare and to recall the needed information, and thus acted as a real timesaver for both the author and the respondent; 3) it allowed the candidates to discuss intelligently the study with their friends and fellow politicians and thus acted as an advance introduction as well as generating a common feeling of assurance as to the purposes of the study.

Although the author always tried to interview each candidate alone, he arrived for several interviews to find the candidate accompanied by

[2] See Cantón, *Argentine Parliamentarians 1889, 1916, and 1946* (M.A. Thesis), p. 168.

one or two of his best friends. The author always began the interview after soon learning that the friends became bored by the questions about social background and soon left. The questionnaire was intended to last about 45 minutes, and the following depth interview was intended to last about fifteen minutes. The interviews averaged about two hours in length because of the difficulty of answering, the tendency of the respondents to give a detailed informational account about party developments which the author already knew, plus the tendency of the respondents to digress repeatedly into the topics which they knew best: party history, party ideology, and the crimes of the opposition political parties. The author was always aware that most candidates expected that the investigator would be interested in these standard topics, probably because most of the political and historical literature in Argentina has been focused upon just these themes.

The author soon developed the habit of dividing the candidates into two groups: the significant party actors, and the not significant party actors. Contrary to most assumptions, the productive Mendocino leads a rushed life rather than a leisurely existence; the tempo of the major political actors is that of a harried person. Thus, the major political actors were men who answered the questions quickly and concisely, and who used their time efficiently out of necessity. With them the interview lasted from 30 to 50 minutes, after which the author had gathered more information than he might get from the succeeding five interviews. The author found these interviews extremely rewarding and enjoyable. The practical rule was that if an interview dragged more than an hour, then the respondent could be considered insignificant in internal party decisions. Politically, such persons are used to fill the electoral ballot and can easily be dismissed as a reliable source of information or as meaningful political actors.

After all the interviews had been completed then the respondents' answers to each question of the standard interview were coded and punched into IBM cards. The codification of the candidates' answers to each question, essentially, consisted of each candidate's own statement. This author, however, attempted (with varying degrees of success) to cross-check each candidate's statements concerning the process of his nomination as a candidate in the depth-interviews with other candidates of the same party. In several instances, consequently, several of the candidate's answers to the questionnaire were altered or modified by evidence gained subsequently. The author depended upon the rule of three to decide if alterations or modifications of any candidate's answers were required: 1) if the respondent's answer correlated with that of three other party candidates, it was accepted as valid; 2) if, however, the respondent's answer or parts of it were contradicted unanimously by three other party candidates, it was altered and codified accordingly. Thus, tables in Chapters III, IV, V contain the statistical information of the modified and unmodified answers to the questionnaire of the 254 interviewed candidates for these public offices from the twelve political parties for the elections of 1962, 1963, and 1965. Basically, the percentages in these tables represent only the candidates' own perceptions; however, that part of the statistics relating to the selection process— although it essentially represents how the candidates perceived the process of their own selection as candidates—does, in many instances, represent the demonstrated evidence as well as the candidates' own perception. No distinction or differentiation, however, between mere personal perception and verified evidence was made in the presentation of this statistical information.

The statistical information in the various tables in Chapters III, IV and V is presented according to the five major party groupings. Necessity demanded the party groupings as the unit of presentation. The reason was that so few interviews were carried out with some individual parties: for example, only two interviews were achieved with members of the Democratic Socialist Party; three interviews were achieved with candidates of the Popular Union Party. To have made any reliable inferences upon the basis of so small a sample would have been impossible. Because the author had to accept this restriction of very few interviews with some parties, a larger unit that the individual political parties is employed; individual political parties are combined into larger units. The party grouping, upon the basis of common ideology, was the logical and convenient choice as the basis of analysis.

This author makes the following suggestions for anyone about to do similar field work studies in Latin America. These suggestions are noted here for several reasons: 1) they are interesting in themselves; 2) they help to indicate better the Mendocino political culture within which the provincial political parties operate; 3) they hopefully will help other investigators to avoid frustrating trials and errors in their field research abroad. This advice is based upon experiences gained from a particular locality in Latin America. The research methods of this study were essentially those of the "trial and error" type, mostly developed after the author was located in Mendoza Province and thus was cut off from his North American friends, neighbors, and academic co-workers. The first suggestion is to have a research design which can be altered, enlarged, narrowed, or changed immediately. This advice would apply even more to survey research than to documentary research in the library.

Originally, this book was to have been an investigation of the recruitment of national deputies by the Popular Radical Civic Union Party in Mendoza Province since the 1958 election. Originally, the study was designed to analyze only the social background and the selection process of about twenty-five national legislative candidates by this one political party. This party was selected because a majority of the relatives of the author's wife were associated significantly in Mendoza Province with this party. Secondly, previous letters to the author from certain party leaders indicated a willingness (and an eagerness by some) to be studied. These plans by the author were made while he was in the United States. When the author had ended his visit to Mendoza Province, he had investigated the recruitment of national and provincial leaders—as well as gubernatorial—candidates from twelve different political parties for the three elections of 1962, 1963, and 1965.

The research design of this study had to be altered and had to be enlarged—contrary to the common advice that field studies be made smaller and more restricted.[3] The fundamental cause was that until the end of the study this author never had the confidence that he could achieve the original goals, and even subsequent aims, of his investigation. After being in the field he decided that he must include several different studies in his research. The purpose was to insure that if the author failed to get the necessary material for one study, he could be sure of completing at least another study and have the minimum of data necessary to complete a book. An examination of the role of achievement-ascriptive factors was included as such a possible substitute. Furthermore, the author carefully examined the political parties' development since 1930 for three reasons. One was to gather necessary background material. Another was to develop a certain "feel" for the province's political parties and political development. A third was to insure that the author could return home with at least enough material to write a history of the political parties, if such was to be his only alternative.

The basic cause for these situations is that this type of study, based upon interviews, by an academician with the present political actors, about contemporary political events had never before been made in the Region of Cuyo. The native political scientists never had done this type of survey research and, in fact, had little contact with the political actors in Mendoza. Both groups tended to regard one another with mutual suspicion. Furthermore, previous political studies had always been of the traditional type of historico-ideological analysis based upon extensive documentary research in libraries. Originally, most politicians assumed that this author would follow this previous pattern. The fact that a North American political scientist was living and studying in Mendoza was itself sufficiently curious. The fact that he was doing survey research was an upsettingly new experience. Added was the fact that this study examined the process of candidate selection, the nerve point of the political party process, and so was possibly dangerous. The

[3] Robert E. Ward, "Common Problems in Field Research," *Studying Politics Abroad,* ed. R. E. Ward and others, pp. 52-53. The author would recommend this book to any person going into a foreign country to do research. The author found many of his own experiences and frustrations noted and examined in this book.

first frustration then was that this type of study had not yet become a part of the "conventional wisdom" of the Mendocino (and of the Argentine) society. Survey research in the United States does not face this obstacle of legitimacy because it has been occurring so long that it is generally accepted by all sectors of society willingly.[4]

One warning is to obtain effective sponsorship from an academic source within the foreign area. When this author did finally obtain a sponsor from the faculty of the University of Cuyo, he found someone who was well respected by the major leaders of all parties, and who was well viewed by the local military leaders. This connection with the military was important. Sponsorship by other academicians might have been meaningless, since they were identified with illegitimate ideological groups. Survey research is a new experience in the less accessible interior areas and thus must first establish its legitimacy. Sponsorship, then, must be by someone who understands the purposes and methods of the study, and whose advice is accepted readily by the local power factors.

Another warning is not to restrict the study, as is commonly advised, to only one political party.[5] This author found that his access to any one party depended upon inclusion of all parties in the study. The Radicals became suspicious and reluctant when they learned that they were originally singled out for examination. For this reason, the author expanded the study to include other parties. Then, everybody seemed to feel more secure knowing that his political opposites were also in-

[4] The condition of being a North American probably intensified, but did not cause, this obstacle of illegitimacy. Argentine socialists also have experienced this same frustration of legitimacy. When Darío Cantón interviewed legislators from the 1946 National Congress, he had to fight relentlessly to get an interview. In conversations with the author, Cantón indicated that both shared many of the same experiences. It is interesting to note that most of Cantón's case studies were members of the 1896 and 1916 National Congresses, whose social characteristics were obtained from biographies and other documentary sources—a difficult, time consuming and scanty source of information. The Peronists were most reluctant to be interviewed by Cantón, ironically an ardent Peronist himself.

De Imaz, in his book *Los que mandan,* did not rely upon the personal interview or questionnaire to obtain information about the social characteristics of the contemporary socio-economic-political elites. Practically all of the information about the political actors was gotten from documentary sources by graduate students in a seminar de Imaz conducted at the University of Buenos Aires. Information on other elites, such as the Church, the military, and the union leaders, was summarized from the internal files of these elites by one of the elite leaders and then given to de Imaz. De Imaz had to rely upon the good will of the elite, who furnished the information in summarized, tabulated form without the use of names or other identifying signs.

[5] Renate Mayntz, "Oligarchic Problems in a German Party District," *Political Decision-Makers,* ed. Dwaine Marvick, p. 141. Mayntz felt that his study was possible because he restricted himself to only the one party, the Christian Democratic Party.

cluded. All candidates of political parties were concerned to know if the Democratic Party's candidates were included in the investigation. Oftentimes, during the initial introductory meeting to arrange for an interview, the prospective respondent would ask if the author had already interviewed the local Democratic candidate. Afterwards, in the interview, this same respondent might severely criticize the Democrats, especially for their conduct during the 1930's. This concern with the Democrats probably stemmed from the fact that the Democrats wielded considerably moral and social influence in Mendocino society because of the socio-economic position accorded them by the popular image. The author did not include the Communists within his research, despite the fact that he wanted to and despite the fact that the major provincial Communist leaders indicated their willingness to be included. The reason was the fear of public reaction: the author was afraid that if he were seen with Communists, political actors of certain other parties would refuse to co-operate.

Foreign fieldwork is done with the absence of those research conditions and devices which are so convenient and are taken for granted in a North American university. The more one gets into the interior, away from the major capital city, the worse these conditions are apt to be. One of the greatest irritations was the absence of basic factual material. The author had to spend much time and energy simply trying to determine simple factual information; whether or not a certain internal election had been held, when an event had occurred, who were the party's officers. Until 1948 the local newspaper, *Los Andes,* was a wealthy source of common factual information about the political parties and political events. Perhaps as a result of the Perón censorship and of the high cost of printing, the newspaper's political activities information was skimpy after 1948. The newspaper's political reporter was, however, a reliable source for checking out dates, names, places, and explanations. Another difficulty was the absence of convenient library facilities for research and study, largely because books and documentary resources are scattered among several different libraries, if they are stocked at all. One irritation was the few hours a day that governmental bureaus and offices are open, so that one's study of certain public sources is chopped into many sessions. Another was that most Argentines hold two or three jobs, between which they must stuff their political activity and any interviews regarding their political activity. The author made most of his interviews from 6:00 to 7:30 A.M. and from 8:30 to 12:00 P.M., and on Saturday afternoons and Sunday mornings. The remainder of the day was spent locating the people, encountering them, and arranging an interview. After sponsorship the difficulty was not so much the unwillingness to be interviewed as the problem of finding a free time in which to make an interview. A very useful device is to develop your own number rule: that is, to pick any number and then use it to multiply or divide the research possibility. Most North American scholars in Argentina use the numbers three or four: if some information is promised within a week, he expects to get it in four weeks; if a certain amount of documentary material is promised, he expects to get only one-fourth of it; and most important, if the author expects to accomplish any intellectual task in accordance with a North American deadline, he automatically extends the deadline four times longer.

If the study had certain irritations, it also included some satisfactions. One was the satisfaction of living in a Latin American society and getting to know its political process and its political actors more intimately than most North American investigators. The Mendocinos are an extremely hospitable people, and in the rural areas the author was generally wined and dined during his visits. This hospitality did not indicate responsiveness in the interview. It oftentimes had its own dangers: if the meal occurred before the interview itself, it often decreased the interviewer's and the respondent's efficiency, especially if the meal included much wine or cognac.

On the whole this author felt that the average Mendocino politician was a dedicated, conscientious person. Personal or economic gain was not an outstanding motive for political participation; and in those few instances where it was apparent, it was only one of several motives. Motives such as the enjoyment of political activity, the desire to assure the representation of certain sectors of society, or the feeling that one could offer meaningful solutions to present problems were stronger. Based upon his own brief experience in Texas politics, this author found the Mendocino politicians to be surprisingly similar.

The last advice is that whereas North Americans may have a bad image among Argentines for being crass, or materialistic, or poorly educated: North Americans also have a good image for being honest, open, and friendly. Instead of being at a complete disadvantage, being a North American may well be an advantage. First, this author felt that the fact that he was a North American assured him access to politicians, documentary information, and certain research privileges which would have been denied to a Mendocino or an Argentine from another province. Second, the author felt that in their relations with him, the Mendocinos tended to emulate those qualities which they imagined and which they respected as being characteristic of North Americans: honesty, openness, friendliness.

The questionnaire used in this investigation is presented as follows:

1) Name of political party ―――――――――
2) Candidacy (position, year, district) ―――――――――
   (and if elected)
3) Party activity of candidate

Party   Party Position Occupied   Years   Department/Province

    3-8 Name the first political party of which you were a member in the beginning.

    3-9 What was your first party post (position elected and/or designated) with this party?

    3-10 Name the other distinct political parties of which you have been a member up to the present.

    3-11 Party positions for which designated?

    3-12 Party positions for which elected?

    3-13 Party positions for which candidate?

4) Public positions of candidate

Party   Public Positions Occupied   Years   Department/Province

    4-1 What was your first public position?

    4-2 Public positions for which designated by the political party?

    4-3 Public positions for which elected as party's candidate?

    4-4 Public positions for which party's candidate?

5) What was the political activity of your grandparents, of your parents, of your brothers, of your children, of your uncles, of your cousins, of your nephews (paternal and maternal)?

Parentage (Relationship only, not names)	*Party*	*Highest Position As*	*Province Department/*
5-1 grandfathers		5-8 prov. deputy	
5-2 parents		5-9 prov. senator	
5-3 brothers		5-10 governor	
5-4 children		5-11 vice-governor	
5-5 uncles		5-12 national deputy	
5-6 cousins		5-13 national senator	
5-7 nephews		5-14 other public position	
		5-15 other party positions	

6) Do you belong to:

    6-1 sport clubs (names)?

    6-2 social clubs (names)?

    6-3 professional associations (names)?

    6-4 civic associations (names)?

    6-5 benefit associations (names)?

    6-6 labor unions (names)?

    6-7 religious associations (names)?

Name of the Associations   *Province*

7) Sex: 7-1 male

          7-2 female

8) Date of birth (month, year)
9) Place of birth:
        9-1 Capital of Mendoza
        9-2 Other department of Mendoza (name)
        9-3 Other province of Argentina (name)
        9-4 Other foreign country (name)

10) Place of birth of mother:
    10-1
    10-2
        repeat choices of No. 9
    10-3
    10-4

11) Place of birth of father:
    11-1
    11-2
        repeat choices of No. 9
    11-3
    11-4

12) Place of birth of paternal grandfather:
    12-1
    12-2
        repeat choices of
        No. 9
    12-3
    12-4

13) Immigration to the province of Mendoza of the first member of your paternal family and year:

13-1	Parentage (relation, not name)	13-6 Before 1900
13-2	Before 1810	13-7 Before 1914
13-3	Before 1852	13-8 Before 1929
13-4	Before 1880	13-9 Before 1944
13-5	Before 1890	13-10 Before 1963

14) Religion: 14-1 Catholic   14-4 Moslem   14-7 Other
              14-2 Protestant 14-5 Orthodox
              14-3 Jew   14-6 Non-denominational

15) The highest level of education finished by: candidate 15————
                                      Candidate's father 15————
                              Candidate's grandfather 15————

15-0	None	15-5 Began university
15-1	Began primary	15-6 Finished university (name
15-2	Finished primary	and title)
15-3	Began secondary	15-7 Other school, institute
15-4	Finished secondary	(name and type)

16) Occupation of candidate (the occupation from which he receives the major per cent of salary)

    16-1 at 21 years   16-4 when a candidate?

    16-2 at 28 years   16-5 occupation of father?

    16-3 at 35 years   16-6 occupation of grandfather?

17) Were you invited to join this party, or did you join voluntarily? (for which candidate)

    17-1 Joined voluntarily?   17-3 Invited by whom (name)?

    17-2 Was invited to join?   17-4 Year joined party?

18) For what reason did you join this party?

19) Name from three to five persons with whom you discuss (or discussed) politics most frequently, or to whom you go (or went) for advice or assistance in your political activity in the year (for which candidate)————————————————————.

Name	*His Position in this Year*	*Party or Group*	*Department/ Province*
19-1			
19-2			
19-3			
19-4			
19-5			

20) Name of three to five of the most important, influential, and powerful members of your political party in the province of Mendoza in the year (in which candidate)————————————————.

Name	*Party Position*
20-1	
20-2	
20-3	
20-4	
20-5	

21) From your political experience within your own party, how would you classify in their order of importance the following causes of internal disputes and of factionalism within the provincial party (rank all in order of their importance):

    21-1 Disputes over ideology and party policy?

    21-2 Disputes over the designation of candidates for the General Election for legislators, aldermen, etc.?

    21-3 Personal disputes between party leaders?

    21-4 Disputes over positions of power within the party?

22) From your political experience within your own party, how would you classify in their order of importance the following causes of

internal disputes between provincial leaders and national leaders of the party (rank all in order of their importance) :

    22-1 Disputes over ideology and party policy?

    22-2 Disputes over the designation of candidates for the General Election for legislators, aldermen, etc.?

    22-3 Personal disputes between party leaders?

    22-4 Disputes over positions of power within the party?

23) Were you solicited to be pre-candidate for (*position for which candidate*) in the year (*for which candidate*)?

    23-1 Not solicited?   23-4 For what reason asked to

    23-2 Solicited?   be a pre-candidate?

    23-3 Name of Persons?   23-5 Name(s) of person(s) that proposed pre-candidate in the party assembly?

24) Name of one to five persons within the party of major importance and decisiveness in your nomination as pre-candidate and as candidate for (position) in the year ——————.

    24-1   24-4

    24-2   24-5

    24-3

25) Do certain pre-candidates or candidates, which represent certain ethnic or social groups, have an advantage to be named candidates for their (your) political party?

    25-1 Have an advantage?

    25-2 Do not have an advantage?

    25-3 Explanation of your reply?

    Is it common or normal for groups outside of the political party to propose pre-candidates within the party? Explain.

    25-4 Is common (propose)?

    25-5 Is not common (do not propose)?

    25-6 Explanation of your reply (how and with examples)?

    Is it common or normal that groups outside of the political party (pressure groups) discharge whatever role in the nomination or the selection of pre-candidates? Explain.

    25-7 Is common (discharge a role)?

    25-8 Is not common (do not discharge a role)?

    25-9 Type of role with examples?

    Name the groups outside of the political party (pressure groups) most decisive in your nomination or election as pre-candidate and as candidate:

    25-10 Name and type of groups (ethnic, related with his profession, social, other)?

25-11 Type of participation?

26) Was there, openly or in a hidden manner, support and/or opposition to your pre-candidacy for (*position for which candidate*) in the year (*in which candidate*) by departmental leaders and how did they demonstrate this support or this opposition?

    26-1   There was support?

    26-2   Who supported (names)?

    26-3   How support demonstrated?

    26-4   There was opposition?

    26-5   Who opposed (names)?

    26-6   How opposition demonstrated?

27) Was there, openly or in a hidden manner, support and/or opposition to your pre-candidacy for (*position for which candidate*) in the year (*in which candidate*) by provincial leaders and how did they demonstrate this support or opposition?

    27-1

    27-2

    27-3

                repeat choices of No. 26

    27-4

    27-5

    27-6

28) Was there, openly or in a hidden manner, support and/or opposition to your pre-candidacy for (*position for which candidate*) in the year (*in which candidate*) by national leaders and how did they demonstrate this support or this opposition?

    28-1

    28-2

    28-3

                repeat choices of No. 26

    28-4

    28-5

    28-6

29) Is it common that national leaders of your party support or oppose a pre-candidate against the decided wishes of the provincial leaders of the party?

    29-1   Rare Situation?

    29-2   Common situation?

    29-3   Explanation of the reason of your reply with examples?

30) Within your own political party, according to its influence and importance in the designation of *precandidates of the party for provincial legislators,* indicate only one answer among those which follow:

30-1 Only the president and official provincial leaders of the provincial party.

30-2 Only the national president and official leaders of the national party.

30-3 Only the departmental president and official leaders of the provincial party.

30-4 Provincial and department leaders of one faction within the provincial party.

30-5 National leaders of one faction within the national party.

30-6 Provincial legislators of the provincial party.

30-7 National leaders of the party from Mendoza.

30-8 Other (explain in detail).

31) Within your own political party, according to its influence and importance in the designation of *pre-candidates of the party for national legislators,* indicate only one answer among those which follow:

31-1 Only the provincial president and official leaders of the provincial party.

31-2 Only the national president and official leaders of the national party.

31-3 Provincial leaders of one faction within the provincial party.

31-4 National leaders of one faction within the national party.

31-5 Provincial legislators of the provincial party.

31-6 National legislators of the party from Mendoza.

31-7 Other (explain in detail).

32) Upon the basis of your experience within your political party, if you had to advise a young man who was interested in a political career in your own party today, in what order would you rank the following personal conditions according to their importance (rank all choices in order of their importance):

32-1 Ability to organize and to discharge a party activity

32-2 Ability to speak in public

32-3 University education, professional abilities

32-4 Strong ideological compromise, that is, penetrated with the party's ideological posture

32-5 Ability to make important friendships within the party and the government

32-6 Ability to organize and discharge a public administrative position

32-7 Family name and antecedents

33) Upon the basis of your political experience, if you had to advise a young man who was interested in a career in a political party

twenty-five years ago, in what order would you have ranked the following personal conditions according to their importance (rank all choices in order of their importance) :

33-1   Ability to organize and to discharge a party activity?

33-2   Ability to speak in public?

33-3   University education, professional abilities?

33-4   Strong ideological compromise, that is, penetrated with the party's ideological posture?

33-5   Ability to make important friendships within the party and the government?

33-6   Ability to organize and to discharge a public administrative position?

33-7   Family name and antecedents?

34) Upon the basis of your experience within your political party, rank in importance the following causes for the influence and the personal progress within your political party today (rank all choices in the order of their importance) :

34-1   Ability to perform favors for the voters

34-2   Constant party loyalty?

34-3   Ability to make and maintain important friendships within the party and the government?

34-4   Ability to organize and to discharge a party activity?

34-5   Family name and antecedents?

34-6   University education, professional abilities?

34-7   Ability to create and fulfill new political programs?

34-8   Ability to organize and to discharge a public administrative position?

35) Twenty-five years ago, how would you have ranked in importance the following causes for the influence and the personal progress within the political party (rank all choices in the order of their importance) :

35-1   Ability to perform favors for the voters?

35-2   Constant party loyalty?

35-3   Ability to make and to maintain important friendships within the party and the government?

35-4   Ability to organize and to discharge a party activity?

35-5   Family name and antecedents?

35-6   University education, professional abilities?

35-7   Ability to create and to fulfill new political programs?

35-8   Ability to organize and to discharge a public administrative position?

36) In what order of importance would you rank the following in-

fluences as determining the vote of provincial and national legislators of your party (rank all choices in the order of importance):

    36-1 The desires of the voters of his district or province?

    36-2 The decisions and attitudes of the official leaders of the party?

    36-3 The party's membership?

    36-4 His own judgment or conscience?

37) Why did you occupy the position number————in the official list of the party for the General Election (*year in which candidate*)?

    37-1 Who determined your position as candidate on the official list (names)?

38) Is it common that provincial leaders of your party support or oppose a pre-candidate against the decided wishes of the departmental leaders of the party?

    38-1 Rare situation?

    38-2 Common situation?

    38-3 Explanation of the reason of your reply with examples?

BIBLIOGRAPHY

Agger, Goldrich, Swanson. *The Rulers and the Ruled.* New York: John Wiley and Sons, 1964.

Alende, Oscar. *Punto de partida.* Buenos Aires: Santiago Rueda, 1965.

Argentina 1930-1960. Buenos Aires: Sur, 1961.

Ayarragaray, Lucas. *La anarquía argentina y el caudillismo.* Buenos Aires: 1925.

———. *Cuestiones y problemas argentinos contemporáneos.* 2 vols. Buenos Aires: L. J. Rosso, 1937.

Bagú, Sergio. *Evolución histórica de la estratificación social en la Argentina.* Buenos Aires: Departamento de Sociología, Universidad de Buenos Aires, 1961.

Barros Hurtado, César. *Hacia una democracia orgánica.* Buenos Aires: Editorial Impulso, 1943.

Beveraggi Allende, Walter. *El partido laborista: el fracaso de Perón y el problema argentino.* Buenos Aires: L. J. Rosso, 1956.

Blanksten, George. *Perón's Argentina.* Chicago: University of Chicago, 1953.

———. "Political Groups in Latin America," *American Political Science Review,* 53 (March, 1959), pp. 106-127.

Burgin, Miron. *Aspectos económicos del federalismo argentino.* Buenos Aires: Hachette, 1960.

Campobassi, José S. and others. *Los partidos políticos: estructura y vigencia en la Argentina.* Buenos Aires: Cooperadora de Derecho y Ciencias Sociales, 1963.

Campoy, Luis. "Conductas diferentes de grupos culturales ante la posesión de la tierra," *Investigaciones en Sociología,* I (1962), pp. 49-83.

———. "Factors that Led to the Successful Revolt of 1930 and the Revolution of 1943 in Argentina." Unpublished research paper. Undated.

———. "Persistencia de algunos valores sociales en una sociedad en desarrollo." Unpublished research paper. Undated.

Cantón, Darío. *El parlamento argentino en épocas de cambio: 1896, 1916, 1946.* Buenos Aires: Editorial del Instituto T. DiTella, 1966.

———. "Parlamentarios argentinos en 1889, 1916, y 1946." Unpublished Master's thesis, University of California, 1963.

Cassinelli, C. W. "The Law of Oligarchy," *American Political Science Review,* 47 (September, 1953), pp. 773-784.

Ciria, Alberto. *Partidos y poder en la Argentina moderna (1930-1946).* Buenos Aires: Jorge Alvarez, 1964.

Coleman and Almond. *Politics of Developing Areas.* Princeton: Princeton University, 1960.

Covarrubias, Ignacio. "El 'Misterio' de Don Gilberto Suárez Lago," *Leoplán,* 26 (April, 1960), pp. 19-24.

Cúneo, Dardo. *Juan B. Justo y las luchas sociales en la Argentina.* Buenos Aires: Editorial Alpe, 1956.

De Imaz, José Luis. *Los que Mandan.* Buenos Aires: Eudeba, 1961.

Del Mazo, Gabriel. *El radicalismo.* 3 vols. Buenos Aires: Ediciones Gure, 1957.

Dickmann, Adolfo. *Los congresos socialistas.* Buenos Aires: La Vanguardia, 1936.

Dirección Nacional de Estadística y Censos, *Segundo censo de la República Argentina.* Buenos Aires: 1898.

————. *Tercer censo nacional.* 10 vols. Buenos Aires: 1916.

————. *Cuarto censo general de la Nación.* 3 vols. Buenos Aires: 1952.

————. *Quinto censo general de la Nación.* 12 vols. Buenos Aires: 1962.

DiTella, Germani, and Graciarena. *Argentina, sociedad de masas.* Buenos Aires: Eudeba, 1965.

Duverger, Maurice. *Political Parties.* London: Metheun, 1951.

Elderseld, Samuel J. *Political Parties: a behavioral analysis.* Chicago: Rand McNally and Company, 1964.

Epstein, Leon. "British M. P.'s and their Local Parties," *American Political Science Review,* 54 (1960), pp. 374-390.

————. "British Mass Parties in Comparison with American Parties," *Political Science Quarterly,* 70 (1956), pp. 97-125.

Fernández Peláez, Julio. *Historia de Maipú.* Mendoza: D'Accurzio, 1961.

Frondizi, Silvio. *Doce años de política argentina.* Buenos Aires: Praxis, 1958.

Galletti, Alfredo. *La política y los partidos.* México: Fondo de Cultura Económica, 1961.

Germani, Gino. "La clase media en la Argentina con especial referencia a sus sectores urbanos," in Crevenna, Theo. R. *La clase media en Argentina y Uruguay.* Washington, D. C.: Pan American Union, 1950.

————. "Clases populares y democracia representativa en América Latina," *Desarrollo Económico,* 2 (July-September 1962), pp. 3-24.

————. *Estructura social de la Argentina: análisis estadístico.* Buenos Aires: Raigal, 1955.

————. *La movilidad social en la Argentina.* Buenos Aires: Departamento de Sociología, Universidad de Buenos Aires, Undated.

————. *Política y sociedad en una época de transición.* Buenos Aires: Editorial Paidos, 1962.

Gil, R. R. *El ex concejal Juan Puebla.* Buenos Aires: Perlado, 1945.

Gómez, Rosendo A. *Argentine Federalism: its theory and practice.* Unpublished Ph.D. dissertation, University of Minnesota, 1950.

Hasseltine, William. *Rise and Fall of Third Parties.* Washington: Public Affairs Press, 1948.

Hernández Arregui, Juan José. *La formación de la conciencia nacional 1930-1960.* Buenos Aires: Hachea, 1960.

Herring, E. P. *The Politics of Democracy.* New York: Norton, 1940.

Jacob, H. "Initial Recruitment of Elected Officials in the U.S.—a Model." *Journal of Politics,* 24 (November, 1962), pp. 703-716.

Instituto de Investigaciones Económicas y Tecnológicas. *Censo nacional de población 1960.* Mendoza: Imprenta oficial, 1961.

————. "Centros poblados de Mendoza," *Estudios Especiales,* 8. Mendoza: Imprenta oficial, Undated.

————. *Esto es Mendoza, 1965.* Mendoza: Imprenta oficial, 1965.

————. "Origen de la población de Mendoza," *Estudios Especiales,* 8. Mendoza: Imprenta oficial, Undated.

Ingenieros, José. *Sociología argentina.* Buenos Aires: Editorial Quipo, 1961.

Iscaró, Rubens. *Origen y desarrollo del movimiento sindical argentino.* Buenos Aires: Anteo, 1958.

Jauretche, Arturo. *F. O. R. J. A. y la década infame.* Buenos Aires: Coyoacán, 1962.

Johnson, John J. *Political Change in Latin America.* Stanford: Stanford University Press, 1958.

Kaplán, Marcos. *La crisis del radicalismo.* Buenos Aires: Praxis, 1958.

Keller, Suzanne. *Beyond the Ruling Class.* New York: Random House, 1963.

Kelly, David. *El poder detrás del trono.* Buenos Aires: Coyoacán, 1962.

Kelsall, R. K. "Social Background of Higher Civil Service," in Robson, W. A. *Civil Service in Britain and France.* New York: Macmillan, 1956.

Key, V. O. *Politics, Parties and Pressure Groups.* New York: Crowell, 1958.

————. *Southern Politics.* New York: Knopf, 1950.

Klain, Maurice. "A New Look at the Constituencies: the need for a recount and a reappraisal," *American Political Science Review,* 49 (1955), pp. 1105-1119.

Lasswell, Harold. "Agenda for the Study of Political Elites," in Marvick, Dwaine. *Political Decision-Makers.* Glenco, Illinois: The Free Press, 1961.

Lasswell and Kaplan. *Power and Society.* New Haven: Yale University, 1950.

Lasswell, Lerner, Rothwell. *Comparative Study of Elites.* Stanford: Stanford University Press, 1952.

Laurencena, Eduardo. *Centralismo y federalismo.* Buenos Aires: M. Gleizer, 1938.

Lazarte, Juan. *Federalismo y descentralización en la cultura argentina.* Buenos Aires: Editorial Cátedra Lisandro de la Torre, 1957.

Lebensohn, Moisés. *Pensamiento y acción.* Buenos Aires: Buenos Aires, 1956.

Leiserson, Avery. *Parties and Politics.* New York: Knopf, 1958.

Levene, Ricardo. *History of Argentina.* Chapel Hill: University of North Carolina Press, 1937.

Leys, Colin. "Models, Theories and the Theory of Political Parties," *Political Studies.* 7 (June, 1959), pp. 127-146.

Linares Quintana, Segundo V. *Los Partidos políticos: instrumentos de gobierno.* Buenos Aires: Editorial Alfa, 1945.

Los Andes (1930-1965). Mendoza: Los Andes, all issues.

Luna, Félix. *Alvear.* Buenos Aires: Libros Argentinos, 1958.

———. *Diálogos con Frondizi.* Buenos Aires: Editorial Desarrollo, 1963.

———. *Yrigoyen.* Buenos Aires: Raigal, 1954.

Macdonald, Austin F. *Government of the Argentine Republic.* New York: Crowell, 1942.

Machado, Daniel Cruz. *Frondizi.* Buenos Aires: Soluciones, 1957.

MacMahon, Arthur W. (ed.). *Federalism, Mature and Emergent.* New York: Doubleday, 1955.

Mafud, Julio. *El desarraigo argentino.* Buenos Aires: Americalee, 1959.

———. *Psicología de la viveza criolla.* Buenos Aires: Americalee, 1965.

Maier and Weatherhead. *Politics of Change in Latin America.* New York: Frederick Praeger, 1964.

Marianetti, Benito. *Problemas de Cuyo.* Buenos Aires: Lautaro, 1948.

———. *Argentina: realidad y perspectiva.* Buenos Aires: Platina, 1964.

Matienzo, J. N. *El gobierno representativo federal en la República Argentina.* Buenos Aires: 1910.

Matthews, Donald R. *Social Background of Political Decision Makers.* New York: Random House, 1960.

———. *United States Senators and Their World.* Chapel Hill: University of North Carolina Press, 1960.

Maupas, Leopoldo. "Trascendencias políticas de la nueva ley electoral," *Revista Argentina de Ciencias Políticas,* IV (1912), pp. 409-428.

Mayntz, Renate. "Oligarchic Problems in a German Party District," Marvick, Dwaine. *Political Decision-Makers.* Glencoe, Illinois: The Free Press, 1961.

McKenzie, R. T. *British Political Parties.* New York: St. Martin's Press, 1955.

Melo, Carlos R. "Las constituciones de la provincia de Mendoza."

Boletín de la Facultad de Derecho y Ciencias Sociales de Universidad Nacional de Córdoba, 27 (1963), pp. 9-162.

————. *Los partidos políticos argentinos.* Córdoba: Universidad Nacional de Cordoba, 1945.

Michels, Robert. *Political Parties.* New York: Dover, 1959.

Ministerio de Gobierno de la Provincia de Mendoza. *Régimen electoral de la provincia: ley 2551.* Mendoza: Imprenta oficial, 1965.

Ministerio del Interior Nacional. *Régimen Electoral Nacional (May 1963).* Buenos Aires: Imprenta oficial nacional, 1963.

Mosca, Gaetano. *The Ruling Class.* New York: McGraw-Hill, 1939.

Naya, Enrique. "La crisis argentina: peronismo y antiperonismo," *Cuadernos,* 43 (July-August, 1960), pp. 45-54.

Neumann, Sigmund. *Modern Political Parties.* Chicago: University of Chicago, 1956.

Oddone, Jacinto. *Historia del socialismo argentino.* 2 vols. Buenos Aires: La Vanguardia, 1934.

Olguín, Dardo. *Dos políticos y dos políticas.* Mendoza: D'Accurzio, 1956.

————. *Lencinas.* Mendoza: Vendimiador, 1961.

Ortiz, Ricardo M. *Historia económica de la Argentina 1850-1930.* 2 vols. Buenos Aires: Raigal, 1955.

Pendle, George. *Argentina.* London: Oxford University, 1961.

Perón, Juan. *Conducción política.* Buenos Aires: Escuela Superior Peronista, 1951.

Potash, Robert A. "Argentine Political Parties 1957-1958." *Journal Inter-American Studies,* I (October, 1959), pp. 515-524.

Puiggrós, Rodolfo. *Historia crítica de los partidos políticos argentinos.* Buenos Aires: Editorial Argumentos, 1956.

Rabinowitz, Bernardo. *Sucedió en la Argentina 1943-1956.* Buenos Aires: Gure, 1956.

Ranney, Austin. *Pathways to Parliament.* Madison: University of Wisconsin Press, 1965.

Real, Juan José. *30 años de historia argentina.* Buenos Aires: Actualidad, 1962.

Rennie, Ysabel F. *The Argentine Republic.* New York: Macmillan Company, 1945.

Repetto, Nicolas. *Mi paso por la política.* Buenos Aires: Rueda, 1956.

Riorden, William L. *Plunkitt of Tammany Hall.* New York: E. P. Dutton, 1963.

Rivero Astengo, Agustín. *Juárez Celman 1844-1909.* Buenos Aires: Kraft, 1944.

Romero Carranza, Ambrosio. *Qué es la democracia cristiana.* Buenos Aires: Atlántico, 1956.

Romero, José Luis. *A History of Argentine Political Thought.* Stanford: Stanford University Press, 1963.

Ross, J. F. S. *Parliamentary Representation.* London: Eyre and Spottiswoode, 1948.

Rowe, L. S. *Federal System of the Argentine Republic.* Pittsburg: Carnegie Institute of Technology, 1921.

Scalvini, Jorge M. *Historia de Mendoza.* Mendoza: D'Accurzio, 1964.

Schattschneider, E. E. *Party Government.* New York: Farrer and Rinehart, 1942.

Scobie, James. *Argentina.* New York: Oxford University Press, 1964.

Selingman, Lester G. *Leadership in a New Nation.* New York: Atherton Press, 1964.

―――. "Political Recruitment and Party Structure: a case study," *American Political Science Review,* 55 (1961), pp. 77-86.

―――. "A Prefactory Study of Leadership Selection in Oregon." *Western Political Quarterly,* 12 (March, 1959), pp. 153-167.

―――. "Recruitment in Politics," *P.R.O.D.,* 1 (March, 1958), pp. 14-17.

―――. "Study of Political Leadership," *American Political Science Review,* 44 (1950), pp. 904-915.

Sigal and Gallo. "La formación de los partidos contemporáneos: la Unión Civica Radical 1890-1916," *Desarrollo Económico,* III (April-September, 1963), pp. 173-230.

Snow, Peter G. *Argentine Radicalism.* Iowa City: University of Iowa Press, 1965.

Sorauf, F. J. *Party and Representation.* New York: Atherton Press, 1963.

―――. *Political Parties in the American System.* Boston: Little, Brown and Company, 1964.

Stokes, William S. "The Centralized Federal Republics of Latin America," in *Essays in Federalism.* Claremont: Claremont Men's College, 1961.

―――. *Latin American Politics.* New York: Crowell, 1959.

Tindaro, C. *Ideario de Juan B. Justo.* 2 vols. Buenos Aires: La Vanguardia, 1939.

Truman, David. "Federalism and the Party System," in MacMahon. *Federalism: mature and emergent.* New York: Doubleday, 1955, pp. 115-136.

―――. *The Governmental Process.* New York: Knopf, 1951.

Vítolo, Alfredo R. "Intervencionismo del estado," *Cuadernos de Proceso,* I (1952), pp. 7-28.

Ward, Robert E. *Studying Politics Abroad.* Boston: Little, Brown, 1964.

Weber, Max. *The Theory of Social and Economic Organization.* London: W. Hodge and Company, 1947.

Wilmart, Raimundo. "El partido radical: su ubicación," *Revista Argentina de Ciencias Políticas,* X (1915), pp. 360-375.

Zorraquín Becú, Ricardo. "La evolución política argentina," *Revista de Estudios Políticos* (mayo-junio, 1949), pp. 159-176.

———. *El federalismo argentino.* Buenos Aires: La Facultad, 1939.

INDEX

THE JAMES SPRUNT STUDIES IN HISTORY
AND POLITICAL SCIENCE

THE JAMES SPRUNT STUDIES IN HISTORY AND POLITICAL SCIENCE

(Continued from inside front cover)